Fairytale
LOVE

How to love
happily
ever after

LEANNE FRENCH

BALBOA
PRESS

A DIVISION OF HAY HOUSE

Interior Graphics/Art Credit: Greg Keith from Wolfies

Balboa Press books may be ordered through booksellers or by contacting:

Balboa Press
A Division of Hay House
1663 Liberty Drive
Bloomington, IN 47403
www.balboapress.com.au
1 (877) 407-4847

Printed in the United States of America.

ISBN: 978-1-4525-1236-5 (sc)
ISBN: 978-1-4525-1243-3 (e)

Balboa Press rev. date: 12/27/2013

To the princesses, queens, princes, and kings in my extended and colourful family. May you all continue to believe in miracles, angels, and happily ever after.

Acknowledgements

I am forever grateful to my beautiful big sister Angela Saari and her delightful daughter Bodine, for reading my finished manuscript and believing in me enough to lend me funds for this project.

I am incredibly blessed to have had a lifetime of unwavering encouragement from my lovely little sister Hayley French. I adore you, Brett, Finley and Ryder, and savour our creative times together where dreams and passions grow in a garden of support.

I am so thankful to my mother Hilarie French for her heart of gold and for all of her love, generosity, and help, especially in caring so well for my son in the days when I was training, travelling, and building palaces. I am grateful to my late nana Dorothy Harnett for teaching her four fabulous daughters, and me, to do our best to change the lives of those who know us.

To kind-hearted Jason, to John and all my other brothers and sisters, nieces and nephews, aunts and uncles, cousins, and friends that have had faith in me to do my life's work, thank you in advance for selling copies and spreading the word!

To my great friend Dr. Clare Murphy, queen of grammar, let me count the ways I appreciate you. Thank you for many years of friendship, and for your help with all of my writing projects in their early stages.

Jared Gulian, author of *Moon Over Martinborough*. Thanks for providing valuable suggestions that culminated in the knitting together of my ideas.

Jared French, my son – *The Little Prince* - I thank you for the miracle you are, and for the look you gave me when you were born that drove me to be the best I could be, for you, for myself, and to others. You are one of my greatest teachers, and I love you enormously. I am so proud of you, your talent, wisdom, and achievements.

To my clients, past, present, and those of you still to come, bless you for believing in my wisdom and letting me work my magic.

Thank you so much to Mary Alvarado and the awesome team at Balboa Press for your brilliance.

Last but never least, giant-size love and eternal thanks goes to my gorgeous, gentle, artistic, inspirational husband Greg Keith. You make my heart sing and my wings soar. I am truly blessed to share my love and my life with you Wolfie.

Contents

Part ONE

Nurturing the Princess Within

On the Way to Happily Ever After...

The story goes like this: Once upon a time, two perfectly matched people got together. Despite misfortune, they pulled out all the stops, didn't hold back, risked, surrendered, had great sex, never got bored, and lived happily ever after.

Sigh. If only it were that easy. Why is it tempting in a relationship of any kind to become complacent, jaded, critical, hurt, or angry? No one expects to experience mayhem or hurtle towards devastatingly destructive futures when we initially pledge our undying fairytale love to each other. The reality is that all couples will experience conflict at some point. It's when unresolved conflict, criticism, contempt, and lack of connection creep in causing disappointment and despair, that the nightmare scenario of an unhappy break-up occurs, brutally destroying dreams and often negatively affecting self-esteem, health, confidence, and even financial standing.

Fairytale Love turns make-believe into "we believe we can make it." With playful transformational tools and proven behavioural-change techniques, you can enrich the love that was there at the beginning, deepen your connection, and strengthen your relationship so that it's healthy, harmonious, love-filled, and lasting. Through affirming, apology, praise, affection, constant care, some miraculous thinking, and a few behavioural adjustments, your dream love can and will return.

Most people just want the same thing. We want to be validated and loved.

We want to see our loved one's eyes light up when we enter the room. We want to know that we can disagree and not be abandoned. We want quality company and as little stress as possible. We want safety and security, compromise and honesty. Sometimes we want it to come with the swish of a magic wand, rather than having to work at it. Life is too short to spend too much time lost in the dark woods, not feeling good inside. This book gives you the magical tools to fix what's busted. It contains solutions and guides you into creating the kind of positive change needed to maintain the love you have and recover everlasting love. It will make it possible for you to choose to see each day as an opportunity to drench one other in kindness.

Just like in fairytales, ordinary life needs imagination. *Fairytale Love* is less about stereotypes of damsels in distress and men saving the day. The following pages are meant to encourage, entertain, delight, and enlighten. Get ready to invent a successful love story, create a wonderful and wild life full of vast riches, and do legendary deeds.

Fairytale Love encourages you to explore and gain insights around why you act in the ways that you do. It teaches you to communicate in a real, respectful, uplifting way, and it playfully lists ways to keep love alive. It will get you questioning your thoughts, feelings, behaviours, values, and beliefs, and just like in fairytales, it's worth considering aspects such as: Is the king or queen fair, does it pay to be grumpy, and what on earth *do* you do if the wolf knocks at the door? *Fairytale Love* is about gallantly following your irresistible, passionate path, even if it means looking hard for the breadcrumbs of hope in a seemingly impenetrable forest. Whilst on your journey, find as much delight along the way as possible, and be guided by a swish or two of my magic wand to unlock the secrets of forever after.

All of the advice contained within, really works. It has been tried and tested by couples in search of relief who have been brave enough to quest and uncover their concerns in therapy with me, over the past twenty-five years. Not only did nearly all of them discover that most problems are solvable, but their romances renewed, fluttered, flourished, and brought them happiness and harmony. There are many reasons why things go wrong, and not enough guidance available on how to make love work. Who teaches you to be a good partner? Where do you learn to love? How do you slay dragons? Most of us learn from what we see, and we could do better. *Fairytale Love* will give you wings to rise above your tangled troubles.

Help is at hand, whether you are already in a great relationship, wanting to know how to maintain the magic, or struggling to delve through difficulties like:

- being obsessed with needing to change your beloved;
- expending too much energy attempting to sway your partner into your way of thinking and feeling;
- anxiously over-focusing on others;
- being overloaded from taking on too much responsibility;
- nagging or whining or being nagged and whined at;

- feeling powerless and negative;
- feeling stuck and a little shocked that things haven't gone the way they were meant to;
- becoming tired of competing for affection and attention;
- feeling insecure or being evasive;
- seething with resentment or self-righteousness;
- being domineering or dishonest;
- trying to avoid yet another marriage meltdown;
- wanting to simply give up;
- having constant arguments with no resolution;
- acting critical and contemptuous;
- feeling sexually frustrated or liable to stray; and
- noticing a deterioration in communication.

Even if your frustration is simply that you can't find the right way to get the end result you want, *Fairytale Love* will help. Who couldn't do with a wise fairy godmother? Sometimes all you need is a gentle reminder, a refresher course, and some simple guidance on how to tweak things so you get a better outcome. The great thing to remember when things aren't going so great, is that:

- Beliefs can be challenged and changed.
- You deserve to live your life fully.
- You are worthy of love and acceptance.

You can accomplish desired change and reach gorgeous goals. You can conjure up more and more acceptable and attractive ways of being. You can soak up the love that is already on offer and get the fizzing sexual spark ignited once again. Approaching difficulties in new ways, and adding delight, can transform any frog into a dream partner once again. Being able to communicate thoughts and feelings in responsible, healthy, caring, conscious, and loving ways really does create the most astonishing results.

My, what big ears you have! If you use them to listen, with a compassionate and open heart, and practise being very much in the present moment, then you will be able to see the innocence and preciousness in your partner, and you can unearth the fulfilment you long for.

My, what a big mouth you have! What you contribute, and most especially, how you do it, can enhance your relationship, maintain meaningfulness, make your life easier, and your days lighter.

That's a lovely basket you have! Sometimes you get what you give, so it's time to learn to give big and acknowledge and treat that amazing human being you share your life with in a supportively delightful way.

Secret number 1: Fun and friendship are the glue that sticks your love together. It's time to live like you are emotionally alive.

Couples that stay together, definitely play together. They fool around in more ways than one! When love and friendship are strong, your beloved will believe in you, even in the moments you forget to believe in yourself. That's a powerful love to have. Live and love in an enriching way and your health and relationship will reap the rewards. Blow your curiosity wide open and get ready to work your laughter lines. Take in what you need and let the rest go.

Secret number 2: Being together needs to be treated like an investment with expected future gains.

What you put in, you get back. Energy flows where intention goes. It's a simple formula. Rather than expecting losses, feed your relationship with positive input so that it can grow, be nourished, and thrive. Your beloved needs to feel competent. Notice and praise his or her positive contributions. Tell your beloved when he or she does things that make you happy, and enjoy the returns from doing so. It's important to believe that it's possible to achieve desired results. Best-selling author Dr. Wayne Dyer has a wonderful saying: "Assume the feeling of the wish already fulfilled." You have the amazing ability to make wishes come true and to make this journey playful, to make it successful, full of rewards, with a good return.

This first part, *Nurturing the Princess Within,* is about accepting yourself and loving yourself, exactly as you are. It can help you fine tune and tweak any dull bits of the brilliant jewel that you are, so that your sparkle dazzles all those who have the pleasure of knowing you.

Secret number 3: Self-love starts with *me*, so that we can build a strong *we*. Think of self-love as the foundation of a happy and full life.

Expect to be delighted, refreshed, and excited along the way as you uncover and understand the finer details of what makes you who you are. Get ready to release any hold the past has on you.

In building terms, it's like defining boundaries. Boundaries are the personal property lines that characterize who we are and what we are responsible for, and they mark out limits and limitations. If you were to consider building a castle, you would:

- investigate;
- explore history;
- understand the lay of the land;
- survey the scene;
- research rules and guidelines; and
- gain a good awareness of possible restrictions.

In relationships, doing the same things gets you better acquainted with where you stand, lets you know what to expect, and gives you vital clues. Knowing where the boundaries are, what's going on around you, and what's inside you, helps you work out what you want and sometimes more importantly what you don't want. With castle building, searching and scrutinizing sidesteps financial ruin, and in relationships we could all do with avoiding costly emotional mistakes.

So:

- gather up your strength;
- put your support systems in place;
- feel excited;
- grab your spade and maybe a modern-day digger; and
- let the inner transformation excavations begin.

Hi ho, hi ho, it's off to work you go.

Awakened Princess

Loving and accepting yourself is a superb start, your first step to really living and loving happily ever after. Doing what you love, having healthy thoughts, being your own best friend, waking up to your wonderful self, and being proud of who you are and what you do, not only increases happiness, it's infectious.

Secret number 4: When you love and accept yourself, it's easier to love and accept others.

The more self-love you have, and the better you cherish and care for yourself, the more awesome and empowered you feel, the more joyful you become. Having healthy, positive attitudes about yourself, who you are, what you are capable of, how you act, and how you look, all help solidify your foundations. Self-love:

- positively influences thoughts, feelings, and behaviours;
- effectively guides you towards accepting and being compassionate towards others; and
- it encircles you with joy, improving the situations and environments you are in.

People who love themselves find it more natural to surround themselves with loving people, uplifting things, and a lifestyle that supports them.

Secret number 5: How you feel about yourself, determines how you relate to others, and how they relate to you.

Most real princesses have too many important things to do, to waste time questioning whether they are good enough. They generally don't get around in slumperdink clothes eating ice cream straight from the freezer in order to numb their feelings. Nor do they take, or allow, negative nonsense from others. At a very young age, they learn to gracefully face the world, to be mindful, courteous and confident, because they know it brings rewards.

Our inner world really does govern a large percentage of our outer world, so it's important we feel good about ourselves. Fill your self-love tanks to overflowing so they can spill over effortlessly. Princesses love to let their brilliance out. Loving yourself is not a selfish act; it's a vital necessity called self-preservation. Purposely giving to yourself, filling yourself up with pleasurable, nurturing things that make you smile and feel fulfilled, can guarantee that you don't operate from a place of emptiness.

Secret number 6: Follow your dreams, and do things that make your heart sing.

Practise gratitude. You can either write down three things you are grateful for from each day or evening, or say them aloud. Find your path, your true north, your passion and your purpose, and know that you are worth the commitment. Don't defer your dreams. Find a way to begin doing what you have always wanted to do. If time and money were plentiful, what would you do with your life? If you won the lottery, what would you do? The more satisfied you feel, the more your happiness increases. Taking responsibility for your personal happiness leads on to naturally contributing to other people's happiness. Happiness is not only about feeling good, it's about living a meaningful life that is full, rich, and interesting. When your authentic self shines brightly, your radiant rays become a beacon that others want to be around.

The first step in loving yourself is to make your own **love list**, so you can refer to it for inspiration. Knowing what makes your heart sing keeps you enlivened, motivated, passionate, engaged, and excited about life. When you create visual, dreamy mood-boards and written reminders, it brings delight and contentment into your world, and banishes boredom forever more.

List five things that you love to do for others.

1.
2.
3.
4.
5.

List five things others do for you, that you love.

1.

2.

3.

4.

5.

List five things that you used to love as a child.

1.

2.

3.

4.

5.

List five things you used to love doing as a child.

1.

2.

3.

4.

5.

List five things you would learn, if you could learn anything.

1.

2.

3.

4.

5.

Here's how it works. What you do for others, and how you do it, is usually a very good indication of what you actually love yourself. Just look at how you shop for gifts. You probably buy other people things that actually delight you. If you love to sit a friend down in front of you and massage away their aches and pains, chances are that you love to be touched. Look at what you are drawn to do for others, what you long to do for yourself on a day off, or what you dream and wish you could do as an extra special treat. Then add those things to your list. The more things you have to choose from, the greater your chance of fulfilment.

Write down:

- possessions you absolutely relish;
- memories that are particularly special to you;
- experiences that make you feel glad to be alive;
- things you just have to indulge in;
- activities that satisfy your soul;
- favourite creative pursuits; and
- wonders that spark your curiosity.

Here are ideas to include and expand on, to get your creativity flowing:

Water, art, films, books, favourite places, shops, clothes, flowers, music, food, drink, beauty, seasonal treats and delights, inspiration, animals, the elements of fire, water, air and earth, travel, dreams, magic, fun, touch, childlike play, exercise, movement, nature, smells, spiritual things, solitude, sanctuary, and comfort.

Plump up your love list with detailed descriptions. I love:

- Collecting nature's beautiful treasure on wild, windswept beaches while listening to waves crashing.
- Snuggling in front of a roaring fire talking about hopes, dreams, and wishes.
- Finding grey striped stones, white pebbles, and heart-shaped rocks.
- Burning candles and oils with citrus essences.
- Eating simple, healthy, delicious food, such as soups, salads, and sushi.
- Meditating in calm quiet places.
- Creating art using gorgeous colours like tangerine, magenta, and turquoise.
- Searching for coloured resin, ribbons, beads, buttons, and craft fabric.

Follow your Bliss

Garden in the rain

SOAK IN AN OUTDOOR BATH FILLED WITH BRIGHT BATH BOMB WATER

Blow bubbles

Fill your house with family, friends, love and laughter

Belly laugh

Create pockets of peaceful beauty on windowsills

Play with magic potions

Throw a dress-up party

Hang an opulent chandelier in a gorgeous space

Be guided by dreams and angels

Listen to music that gives you goose bumps

Seek your tribe

PLAN YOUR WONDER-FILLED PATH TO A FABULOUS FUTURE

Embrace your inner mermaid

Befriend a witch

Believe

Embrace Your Majesty

Loving yourself is about consciously choosing to be nice to yourself and rewarding yourself when you do things well. You can amplify self-love by taking pride in your achievements. You can also boost your self-esteem by lovingly promising to view yourself in a more positive light. Feeling good about the things you do and remembering to give yourself credit for what you have already done, instead of worrying about what you have yet to do, is a wonderful habit to get into.

Own all of your wonderful, shining successes.

Acknowledge how magnificent, brilliant, gorgeous, talented and fabulous you are. Include:

- certificates gained;
- exam marks;
- presentations;
- awards;
- work that sold;
- amazing things you have made;
- children born, adopted, fostered, or cared for;
- parties held;
- associations formed;
- sports played;
- memberships held;
- times you were sought after;
- skills you have;
- races run;
- goals met;
- friendships kept, friendships made, and difficult friendships you courageously let go of;
- truths told;
- rifts that you have healed; and
- everything else you can think of that you have excelled at.

Secret number 7: What other people think of you is none of your business.

Feeling majestic is enhanced by concentrating more on what you think and do, rather than worrying so much about what other people think of you. We don't have to let the opinions of others affect us. It's just not worth trying to do the right thing, or be the right person, to suit someone else or make him or her like us. Remember this: You don't have to like everybody, and not everybody will like you. Taking things personally, worrying, and adapting, drains us of energy and causes undue stress that takes up too much precious space in our minds and hearts. We need to free ourselves from second-guessing and over-analysing. Byron Katie, speaker and author of *The Work* puts it beautifully. "What I think and what I feel is my business. What you think and what you feel is your business. When I'm worried about how you feel about me, I'm in your business. And if I'm busy living in your business, how am I present for my own business?"

Secret number 8: The disease to please usually stems from a fear of conflict, the need for approval, and the fear of rejection.

Overly pleasing others can be emotionally exhausting and has a tendency to pull us in all directions, except the one that propels us forward. Learning to put ourselves forward, and beginning to pay attention to what it is that we need to do to please ourselves rather than others, increases energy.

Never diminish yourself or dull your sparkle in order to be with another.

More often than not, be willing to step up and into an equal footing, resist the urge to fade away, and refuse to scuttle around in the shadows plumping up the cushions of content for others.

Listen to the Whispers Within

Secret number 9: Everyone has an intuitive sense of what path or action they could take.

Our unconscious always tries to find ways to be heard. We just need to slow down enough to listen and notice. Whenever you feel lost, directionless, worried, or unable to sleep, just:

- slowly breathe deeply into your belly;
- calm your thoughts and turn your attention to bodily sensations; and
- search for the whispers within.

Banish all the inner should, must, and have to messages and instead choose to tell yourself you can.

Wisdom whispers calmly. It sometimes appears as emotional or physical sensations in our body. When we purposefully look and ask the universe for guidance, answers can show up as synchronicity and co-incidence. Whispers speak from our unconscious and they surface in our nightly dreams. Whispers contain solutions to our questions and they allow our daydreams to bubble to the surface. Throw all of those meaningful messages into a cauldron. Mix in a dash of intuition, add a dose of practicality, and stir well until clarity appears. Boil down until decisive choices that stem from a deeper knowing emerge, and you will be magically nudged forward on your path. Whispers of wisdom gently guide us towards the kinds of friends and teachers that suit us best. They cajole us in the right direction. Rather than question the direction, it's helpful to remember that the universe often has a plan for us that's bigger than the one we have for ourselves.

Sometimes the answers we are looking for jump out from the words in a book, in lectures or conversations, or even in a feeling received from an animal or stranger. Jungian psychoanalyst Dr. Clarissa Pinkola Estes believes that unusual characters in fairytales disguise their divinity to test us, to see if we recognize the greatness of soul in various forms. She says, "They show up in robes, rags, silver sashes, or with muddy feet. They show up with skin dark as old wood, or in scales made of rose petal, as a frail child, as a lime-yellow old woman, as a man who cannot speak, or as an animal who can."

Time in the Tower

Physical and emotional solitude is splendidly beneficial for the renewal and healing of our minds, hearts, and souls. Towers are symbolic places to go to, to set things right. When we position ourselves in quiet places away from dastardly distractions and duties, we rise above difficulties and reconnect with our essence. That's when helpful creative ideas begin to effervesce. If we can capture them spilling over, they add fizz and serve to remind us how to re-engage sumptuously with life.

The most brilliant way to get time-out is to willingly surrender into peace-filled opportunities. Better that, than to have some tyrant imprison us in a locked turret. Being forced to spend time alone takes the fun out of it. What we really want to avoid is an evil witch arriving in the form of an illness if we refuse to slow down our hectic schedules.

Silence clears away rubble, calms the critic, steers us away from negativity, helps us soar, and eases the crushing pressure of an overloaded life. What you do with the peace and serenity is up to you.

You could:

- simply let down your golden-hair and brush it with one hundred strokes;
- use the time to craft your imagination;
- make a ball gown;
- talk to a unicorn;
- seek beauty;
- catch up on lost sleep to renew your spirit;
- read a tall tale;
- sit in the shimmering sun on a summer afternoon;
- dabble in the tarot;
- polish your gold; or
- soak in a bath filled with bubbles.

Hang signs on your door that read:

- Taking space, not available until recharged.
- Self-care in progress, please do not disturb.

Make space in your day for snippets of sanctuary:

- Put a lock on your bathroom door if others are always busting in.
- Avoid rush hour.
- Stay away from loud chatter.
- Don't buy into the sense of urgency in the world.
- Go to cafes between eleven and twelve, if that's their least busy time.
- Find the quietest time to visit your local swimming pool or gymnasium.
- Shop on stormy, rainy days when others don't dare venture out, or better yet, shop online and support artisans and small businesses.
- Have absolute work-free days when you don't talk about work, don't read about work, and don't even think about work.
- Let your answer-phone pick up your messages from time to time.
- Have a set time that you check your email messages and social media, to avoid overload.
- Say no to junk mail.
- Make a pact to only handle your mail and paperwork once.
- Learn to say no to requests for your time that don't feel right.
- Demonstrate good management, delegate and surrender when you can.
- Manage your money. Avoid getting into unnecessary debt.
- Have it be okay to seek expert help if something feels beyond your capabilities.
- Keep your life and surroundings as clutter-free and tidy as possible. A good rule of thumb is that whatever you get out, you put back.
- Hire a cleaner for an occasional treat.
- Seek expansive wide-open spaces.
- Remember that actions have consequences, and chaos and drama are best avoided.
- Surround yourself with people who support you without judgement. It keeps your headspace a lot clearer.

Release Your Inner Princess

- Exude confidence.
- Practise serenity.
- Make room for the divine.
- Soak up silence.
- Be positive.
- Let go of regrets.
- Don't make assumptions.
- Pamper your skin.
- Be passionate.
- Recharge now, not later.
- Treat yourself.
- Nurture your creativity.
- Smell scrumptious.
- Embrace loyalty and sincerity.
- Spend quality time with excellent friends.
- Be charitable.
- Sniff wildflowers.
- Set healthy boundaries.
- Laugh heartily.
- Melt away your troubles in candle-lit baths or fragrant showers.
- Sing, dance, and move your body.
- Indulge in small luxuries.
- Keep everything simple.
- Express yourself.
- Be impeccable with your word.
- Speak your truth often, even if your voice shakes.
- Throw out your raggedy undies, gowns, and cloaks.
- Use your best china.
- Be charitable and donate goods you really don't need.
- Always do your best.

How to be Utterly Charming

In an ancient version of *Sleeping Beauty,* the princess awakens and tells the prince he has kept *her* waiting a long time. He was really the one who was mesmerized, charmed, and won over by her sassy, confident words which undoubtedly originally inspired the term Prince Charming. Using charm is like exercising magical powers. Charming people give out love and make others feel special. They listen carefully, are optimistic, and pleasant to be around. Be your own kind of beautiful and emanate kindness, warmth, and thoughtfulness. It will enliven and brighten the lives of others.

Foster charming ways of being:

- Always wear an invisible crown.
- Put your shoulders back.
- Walk tall.
- Remember that compliments will get you far.
- Use the magic words please and thank you.
- Swoop to open carriage doors for those who have their hands full.
- Be compassionate and kind-hearted.
- Let your brilliance burst forward.
- Compliment yourself, it reduces self-criticism and comforts the child within.
- Believe in your positive strengths and enchanting qualities.
- Champion the talents of others.
- When engaging in conversation, use tactful touch.
- Smile, and let your warmth light up the room.

Make affirmations a part of your world and practise make believe:

- ✓ I am enough. I have enough. I do enough.
- ✓ I can be fully who I am in the presence of others, no matter who they are or what they believe in.
- ✓ I am loving and loveable.
- ✓ I am filled with love and affection.
- ✓ I am healthy and joyous.

- ✓ I deserve the very best that life has to offer.
- ✓ I trust my perceptions.
- ✓ I am true to myself.
- ✓ I can say yes to my desires.
- ✓ I speak my truth.
- ✓ I am richly rewarded.
- ✓ I radiate success, and I prosper wherever I turn.

Affirmations may seem simplistic, yet they have a wonderful way of turning around any negative thoughts that lurk in our depths, and they drive our thoughts and behaviours. Affirmations help us believe in our positive potential, encourage us to shine, and make it easier to be less afraid of showing our optimistic self to the world.

Trust your perceptions.

- Be true to yourself.
- Be willing to change.
- Say yes to your desires.
- Speak your authentic truth.
- Pay attention to what *is* working in your life.
- Look for good news.
- Stay away from negative influences.
- Seek things that fuel you.
- Stay away from things and people that drain you.
- Be positive and have hope in your heart.
- Help yourself and let others help you.
- Release the past and refuse to dwell on what you don't want.
- Look at what you do want. Dig it up. Let it out.
- Seek fulfilment.

Loving what you do makes charming conversations much easier to have. When you have a lot to offer, relationships have an astonishing tendency to thrive. The more loving your thoughts are, the more harmonious, peaceful and balanced you become. When you experience joyous thoughts and feelings, charming and happy chemical surges are released into your body, and so the positive cycle continues.

Sleeping Beauty

Sleeping Beauty has a number of underlying warnings that analysts like to bring to our attention. They talk about it being a cautionary tale, one that discourages women from broadcasting or enjoying the onset of blossoming sexuality. Perhaps the tale was also designed to deter us from straying, disobeying, and playing with sharp spinning wheels in dusty attics. Even though we know that punishment (usually by a sharp prick) is always possible, who doesn't like to rebel now and again? Those key elements however are not as memorable as the image of the prince battling his way through tangled thorny bushes to get to the sleeping princess who was waiting for his passionate kiss to bring her back to life. Thank goodness for equality where women don't have to rely on being rescued. We don't even have to be pleasured by someone else. In modern times, we can just about give ourselves most things.

How often are we like a sleeping beauty, sleepwalking through our days, our duties, our work, our relationships, in fact our lives? Put your hand up if you fall victim to dulling yourself, if you fail to notice lush interesting activities that surround you. Do you walk past spiky flora and fauna and forget to marvel at its beauty? When chirping birdsong fills the air, do you stop and listen?

Mind-numbing, monotonous, dreary days are one thing, but staying asleep to the joys life has to offer, can have dangerous consequences. It's a tragic waste when a young woman marries and feels she has to give herself over to her husband, unknowingly sacrificing her dreams, needs, or even a career to ensure that her husband is more important. Worst of all, she may somehow consider herself his property. Then there are other women, who think their partners should just magically supply them with everything they need, like love, company, conversation, wealth, and terrific tea parties, and are shocked to discover it's not sustainable. They may need to wake up to themselves!

If you are waiting to be kissed into life, forget it.

Relationships may only provide up to eighty percent of what we need (if we are lucky) no matter how fabulous our partner is. Realistically no one can ever give us everything.

Waiting around for that absent twenty percent is like *Sleeping Beauty* waiting for the ultimate kiss to wake her up. It could take a very, very, long time. Satisfaction in love comes a lot easier when we are able to take responsibility for meeting our own needs.

The great thing about being conscious of our thoughts, feelings, and behaviours, is that it keeps us in touch with our needs. If you feel taken for granted or recognize that you have been giving too much, take some time to clearly identify what you think is going on, even if you have to write it down.

If you hear yourself complaining about being exhausted, or you feel swamped by demands, don't wait to be rescued. Nothing is likely to change until you make it happen. Increasing awareness around the choices you make and remembering that they are indeed choices, is helpful. You choose your actions, and your words. All actions and words have consequences. Rather than getting angry, how about acknowledging any hurt you may feel. Do you have to give so much or do so much? Could you say no, and survive? Could you be more specific in your requests? Could you gently, kindly, ask for what you need?

Unfortunately not all good things come to those who wait. It's much better to set your alarm clock and get up and out there, fully awake, to see if you can identify what you are missing. Stay waiting and there is a chance you could feel scratchy, unfulfilled, and needy.

Identify the absent twenty percent or more by pondering these questions:

- What do I want?
- If I got what I wanted, what feeling would it give me?
- What am I going to have to do, in order to get what I want?
- How will I feel when I have it?
- How will I know when I've got it?

Waking up to ourselves can mean giving up the once upon a dream my life will be perfect mentality. It's completely acceptable to trip up, fall, and even fail now and again. It's also okay to put yourself first, to maximize your potential, and propel yourself forward. Rather than shielding your fabulous self from the outside world, why not get out there amongst it? How about starting a group and giving it a fun name? You could meet at a time that is suitable and easy for everyone. It could be in person, or online. Decide what you'd like, what works for you, and bravely do it. The purpose of the group is to fulfil that twenty percent. It could be a group designed to talk about your feelings, to exercise, to pole dance to get in touch with your sexy self, to reveal your innermost ideas in safety, or it could be a creative group where you are productive. The main idea is to get what you need for yourself in an empowered way, to stop any resentment creeping in, and to reduce blame if you feel that your beloved isn't doing enough.

If you're not the group type, you may want to get your twenty percent met through various friends. It's good to connect with others who enjoy the same kinds of things as you. You can still go to art house movies and talk in depth for hours afterwards even if your beloved will only watch documentaries. Shopping buddies could join you cruising fabric stores and craft fairs. You could find someone to ride your bike with, or partner you in the gym, or on a court. Just because your beloved doesn't have all the same interests as you, or may not be interested in yours, doesn't mean you can't, or shouldn't, indulge your interests. Nor should you feel like *having* to do what your beloved does. As long as your friendships have good safe boundaries, then go ahead and have fun.

Give what you most want to get:

- If you continue to feel like something is missing, how about being willing to try a whole new approach? Identify the problem, find a positive equivalent, and behave in exactly that way towards your beloved. If for example you feel ignored and rejected, choose to give up that feeling by behaving and acting more supportive and welcoming. Just do it, and see what happens.
- If you feel like you aren't getting touched enough, initiate the touching.
- If you are annoyed by the lack of conversation coming your way, you do the talking and asking. Find interesting topics to chat about.
- If you want better sex, get sexy. Find a way to turn him or her on. You make the moves and direct the action.
- If you want more adventure and excitement, book an activity.
- If you want fun, bring home a movie that's guaranteed to make your eyes water in a good way. Whip out a board game after dinner.
- If you want to be treated like you are special, let him or her know how important they are to you. Let your uniqueness shine, and keep building a self that's not dependant on anyone else.

- If you desire to have your cleverness noticed, keep saying intelligent things, and aim to feel worthy simply because you are.

The unfortunate thing that can happen if we believe we aren't getting particular needs met, is that we might behave badly and attract less than fabulous responses. This in turn can increase unpleasant feelings and reinforce our bottom line, boring, and untrue negative beliefs. Feeling punished or inflicting self-punishment, has a tendency to recreate original pain from our past. Whatever positive feeling we want more of, we need to do it and be it, and we will get it. We just have to push through any resistance and give what we want to get. If we stay away from victim behaviours and choose to be an active empowered part of the solution, we stand a better chance of creating positive experiences. Just remember you want change, you want results, so think of what you have to gain, and be the change you want to see.

Try taking a day or two where you mostly focus on your own needs. It's not always about going over the top and shutting everyone out for one hundred years.

- Go on a mini retreat.
- Reduce all areas of giving for a set period of time.
- You could start with one hour, one day, one week, or maybe even one year if you really want to go wild.

Sleeping Beauty symbolizes passivity and non-action. We on the other hand, are able to meet our own needs and ensure that we are properly resourced. Are we eating, sleeping, drinking, and nurturing adequately? Are we resting sufficiently? Could we learn to be less available and maybe move away from being on call for others? There is always a way to find someone who can help should we decide to take a break from family or work commitments. When we aim for rejuvenation and revival, we reduce tiredness. Reducing tiredness ensures we don't end up snapping, speaking disrespectfully, or pricking everyone else with a sharp tongue.

- Hear your own wisdom when you speak.
- Seek nature, moonlight, and beauty.
- Inhale the aroma of coffee.
- Lick peanut butter off a spoon.
- Soak up love like sunshine.
- Sniff the fragrance from a rose, being very careful to avoid poisoned thorns.

Secret number 10: Ask yourself this at least several times a day: What do I need to do to care for myself right now?

Write down secret number ten and carry it around in your pocket. Wait for, listen to, and respect your answer because your feelings are your truth. Sometimes the answers may be simple, like ask for a hug, eat sushi, drink water, and smile. Other times answers such as walk away, don't react, or let it go; can get you out of a pickle.

Even when we get what we need, sometimes we aren't very practised at receiving. It helps to say thank you and mean it and to welcome praise rather than brush it off. Don't look for a hidden agenda when you are being offered love, just put your hand on your heart, smile, and lap it all up graciously.

Secret number 11: When you praise others for doing good and meeting your needs, chances are they will do their best to keep meeting them.

The prince woke the princess with a perfect kiss. Our loved ones may not always do the right thing or be eternally faultless, but more often than not he or she will show us love in many ways. Even if the signposts of love are subtle, or non-verbal, it's our job to take notice and to praise and thank them for it. Love is a doing word, so let's be willing to look at what *is* being done.

- Watch for that certain look that is reserved just for you.
- Enjoy being held in the middle of the night.
- Know that when he or she laughs at your jokes, even the lame ones, they do it because they love you.
- Remember that reminiscing is love rekindled, and he or she has gone to an effort to make you feel good.
- Capture compliments and feel content. Give a compliment back.
- When someone says something nice about you in front of others, say thanks.

Secret number 12: True love is worth staying awake to feel. It conquers all. Even curses.

The Frog Prince

In the tale of *The Frog Prince*, a spoilt princess reluctantly befriends a frog and tries offering him riches. Riches are not high up on his priority list. Like most emotionally healthy princes who are searching for love, he wants a real and direct relationship. In her impatience, the princess hastily promises him what he wants, mostly so he will just hurry up and return her precious golden ball from the deep pond. When she gets what she wants, the princess selfishly brushes him to one side and runs off to play. The frog eventually comes looking for her, and that's when she is made to keep her word. The frog then eats from her plate and sleeps on her bed, much to her moaning and disgust. On the third night, it becomes apparent that the princess is actually capable of having a pure and loving heart the moment she kisses him on his little cold wet frog nose. Her kiss broke the spell the frog was under, and like all good and hopeful fairytales, the frog turned back into a handsome prince and they lived happily ever after.

How interesting that the princess just went ahead and made a contract with a stranger, without adequate consideration. How often do we do that? Did she even consider the effects and consequences of making such a promise?

How many times have we all rushed headlong into deals, friendships, or relationships, only to find out a little later down the track that it was a bad idea? How many times have we uncovered bullies in disguise, con artists, or people with ways or opinions that don't resonate with our values, making them hard to tolerate?

Or maybe like us, the spoilt princess thought that frogs and royalty pairing up together in a story was a little weird to begin with?

On one level, the tale of *The Frog Prince* directs us towards the idea that we each have shadow parts of ourselves that we can occasionally look at in disbelief and shock. One morning at least, it's possible that we will wake up next to our loved one feeling disillusioned or slightly repulsed. Maybe they are going through a time of self-searching that we find boring. Maybe redundancy, or their earning capacity has altered and affected not only how they feel, but also how we see them. It could be that depression, grieving, aging, balding, weight-gain, or weight-loss creeps us out. Then there's the stock standard irritation. He or she may call us to task on *our* less than fabulous behaviours, and in doing so suddenly seem unattractive. That's when the urge to brush them off can seem overwhelming, and make us want to run screaming. Those are in fact the times to act less spoilt and more real. In most situations it pays to remember to listen and receive feedback graciously, to be compassionate, accepting, and know that to err is human.

It only takes a shift in focus to remember that slimy suitors are usually gorgeous hunks in disguise, and that they are just as vulnerable as we are, with ever-changing exteriors.

Great things often hide in unsuspecting skin.

Change involves moving away from feeling disillusioned. If you believe that receiving love has to look or feel a certain way, is it possible that you're not comfortable with spontaneity or imperfection? Imperfection allows room for vulnerability, and vulnerability draws people closer; it's what connects us all.

- Do you put tough rules on yourself?
- Do you have strict guidelines around how others are supposed to be?

Rigidity has an annoying habit of covering up vulnerability and it makes intimacy difficult. If you notice yourself becoming rigid, why not try softening? Remember that loved ones aren't always going to co-operate, so how about planning new ways of responding in challenging circumstances.

You could:

- count to three;
- remove yourself from the room;
- sing a song in your head to distract yourself from having to respond; or
- just say aloud that it is okay to agree to disagree.

Try not to focus on a perceived lack of support. Deep resentment can build if we feel like we aren't receiving the kind of love we want or expect from our partner.

Those who wait to be loved in the right way before they love back are more likely to end up in a loveless standoff.

Instead of feeling ripped off, unsupported, neglected, or unworthy, we could instead consider examining our answers to the following:

- What am I neglecting and what can I do about it?
- Are there things that I need to notice in others and myself that I am not paying attention to?

There are clear consequences that show up when we don't give ourselves what we need. Some people end up craving deep, dark wells to hide in. Others become exhausted. Do it for long enough and molehills could reach mountainous proportions.

In order to protect your sensitive self, it may be a good idea to consciously stay away from shady, hostile, aggressive types. Avoid people with active addictions, and those who are either completely shut down or overly involved in their own existence. It may also be a good idea to steer clear of hanging around with warty toads!

Frogs are sensitive little critters. They are also incredible indicators of the health of our environment. Like us, they need physical safety and emotional kindness.

When we keep our promises to frogs, others, and ourselves, it makes us more approachable and better able to meet the needs of others.

The tricks to staying resourced include:

- increasing self-care;
- maintaining balance;
- remembering to breathe low and slow, deep down in the belly; and
- having an open willingness to fill life with people who are fun, emotionally available, willing generous spirits with high creativity and plenty of inspiration.

Be interesting.
Be an inspiration.
Be the 'get up
and go' that
you are
looking for.

Who is the Fairest of Them All?

This saying came from a simple fairytale about a caring mother who gave birth to a beautiful daughter with black hair, white skin, and red lips whom she named *Snow White*. When *Snow White* was seven, her mother died. That's when her father got married again, to a queen with an unfortunate anger management problem. The queen didn't like being surpassed in the beauty department, so when her magic mirror told her one too many times that *Snow White* was the fairest of them all, she flew into an envious, jealous rage so violent, that she ordered a hit-man huntsman to rip the little girl's heart out. The huntsman became so smitten by the beauty and innocence of *Snow White* that he couldn't go through with it. *Snow White* turned into a teenage runaway and went into hiding. The queen eventually hunted her down and found her living a humble and hardworking life at the street-smart seven dwarves house, deep within a forest. The queen attempted to murder *Snow White* three times, each time playing on vanity and trickery. Once she cleverly used laces and a comb as temptation, knowing full well that most girls are naturally drawn to fashion and beauty. The last murder attempt fortunately only resulted in a prolonged sleep in a glass coffin. When the piece of poisoned apple became dislodged, *Snow White* woke from her long slumber and married the prince that rescued her. They lived happily ever after. The queen, not so much! She was forced to wear magic red shoes that made her dance until she dropped dead.

Mirrors aren't just for vanity, they are instrumental in allowing us to see ourselves, and can represent the way others see us. Whatever answer we imagine, to the question, "Who is the fairest of them all?" is really just the voice of judgment that rules women's self-evaluation.

The queen clearly envied the beauty and sex appeal that *Snow White* possessed, and she had difficulty accepting her own age. Her competitive edge, mixed with a fearful belief that she may not be able to keep a man if and when her looks faded, were an invitation to lose control.

Looking and asking for reassurance of beauty without remembering to build a strong sense of self that celebrates other important things like talent, smartness, and wisdom, is unwise.

We as women could do with finding ways to be accepting of others and ourselves, even though we are bombarded with a somewhat destructive mirror of society.

There is unfortunately such intense pressure to conform to an ideal standard. Something is wrong when our culture puts perfection, youthfulness, and how we should look up on a pedestal, and yet every day it challenges all of us. We need to *see* that not all is right with this picture. An incomplete sense of self can invite dissatisfaction and encourage unwelcome feelings of not being good enough.

Secret number 13: Uncertainty is what makes life joyful and interesting. Perfection and rigidity squish the living daylights out of beauty.

It's also as shallow as a magic mirror to expect perfection from another human. It would be very villainous indeed if we all thought that we could only be with someone who has the ideal bank balance, weight, or a full head of hair. Expectations need to be fair and based around personality traits, qualities, and emotional capability. When we stay open to the possibility of change, and accept the ups in a relationship as much as the downs, it encourages flexibility. It's advantageous to see the pearl of wisdom in gritty situations. When we find the confidence to manage change, it's easier to believe that others are capable of doing the same.

Secret number 14: Love is full of surprising discoveries when you cultivate your capacity to be kind, compassionate, and loyal.

Embrace the notion that good usually triumphs over evil. Aim to be as kind to others as you would like him or her to be to you. Reasonable expectations include:

- appreciating differences and lovingly resolving difficulties;
- sharing concerns, ideas, hopes, and dreams;
- discussing direction and priorities; and
- not lusting after a life that mirrors anyone else's.

"Perfection is achieved not when there is nothing more to add, but when there is nothing more to take away."
Antoine de Saint-Exupery.

Make Friends with Monsters Under Your Bed

Who remembers sleeping with their hands and feet inside the bed as a child, rather than over the edge, just in case some random monster took the opportunity to pull you under into the darkness?

Life is crammed with monsters crouching at the door pretending to be friends, partners, and sometimes in-laws. Fairytales are filled with child-eating witches and wolves to perhaps warn us of the danger that some people are here to protect us, and others have the ability to hurt us. From a Jungian perspective, if all parts of a fairytale in some way represent parts of the self, then we also have the capacity to be protective or harmful to others and ourselves. Never mind the world being a frightening place, our subconscious is more than likely filled with terror and confusion, along with mischief and desire. Better that we make friends with all of it.

Our core self is made up of our earliest feelings, memories, and belief systems. These have, and continue to have an effect on our experiences. Just as our physical body has been shaped and moulded by historical and hereditary factors, so too have the intellectual, sexual, spiritual, and emotional parts of us.

The more we know about our wounds, joys, pains, and pleasures, the more we can begin to appreciate whether they serve us or not. It's really beneficial on the journey of self-awareness to know how they got there, recognize what their purpose is, and know how they influence our thinking, feelings, and behaviours.

Collective problems often need individual solutions. The most brilliant way to gain information is to use our amazing imaginations and talk to the monsters. What they say can help us come up with healing strategies, options, and secure solutions.

If your dreams fill with nightmares, especially repetitive ones, converse with the monsters about the things that threaten you. You can do this by either writing about it, or acting it out. It's about giving the dark nature a voice rather than discounting it, which can open the door to wonderful insights and creativity. The things those monsters say can be amazing, funny, and extremely insightful. Perhaps the man or critter or monster chasing you in your dreams just needs asking *why* when you wake up. He may turn out to be a messenger of wisdom and surprise, present in your unconscious to inform you about something of importance.

A viewing of an art show that showcased Niki De Saint Phalle's "Queen Califia's Magical Circle," which had an incredibly beautiful sculpted wall of playful mosaic serpents slithering along the top, was a fine example of transforming unconscious monsters by bringing them to life artistically. According to the artist's granddaughter, Niki wouldn't stay in bed as a child, so her father told her the floor was covered in snakes. Bringing those snakes back, larger than life, and in a playful way in her artwork, was perhaps her powerful way of refusing to be frightened.

Tim Schaefer, Gamer and Founder of Double Fire Productions was named one of the most creative people in business in 2012. When interviewed for Fast Company, he had this to say about monsters: "Every day, we think of crazy ideas and then we laugh and say, 'People might be offended by that' or 'People aren't expecting that from me.' But I have found that everything worth doing is hiding behind a big, scary monster." When asked what inspiration outside of gaming did he find most valuable, he had this to say: "I love studying folklore and legends. The stories that people passed down for a thousand years without any sort of marketing support are obviously saying something appealing about the basic human condition."

Secret number 15: Problems and fears can be opportunities. You can reclaim, begin to heal, and move towards freedom of choice when you are in charge of your emotions.

Go ahead, open the door to your crazy ideas and be willing to be transformed. Peek under your bed, and welcome what you find. Be prepared to uncover things without being scared of them, because in reality, those things you try to stay away from may find ways to unleash themselves anyway. When you shine a torch into the darkness there's usually nothing to actually be afraid of. Unless, under your bed, along with the odd lost dirty sock, you find a lot of unpaid overdue bills and some very, very, large toenail clippings.

Dealing with Dragons

"It does not do to leave a live dragon out of your
calculations if you live near him."
J.R.R.Tolkien.

Sometimes the dragon lives within, and often it's no surprise when our fire escapes and we either get burnt, or singe others. Knowing how the dragon got there, why it hangs around, and when it's likely to strike, can make our life and relationships a lot easier. Knowing how we tick invites greater self-control. With greater self-control comes less conflict.

Emotional healing is much like peeling away the layers of an onion. An onion is an image that suggests that there is always a deeper level to work on, to uncover, to expose. It also suggests it will usually make us cry. What's completely interesting is that it's often exactly the same original wound that resurfaces over and over. We just get to the same core, in different ways, time and time again.

You will know if a pattern is repeating itself if your pain, hurt, and suffering touch in on your belief systems and feel overly familiar.

There are four levels where an original wound infiltrates and each level affects your thinking, feelings, and behaviour. An original wound acts much like a fire starter.

The difficulty that many people face, is they cannot see that how they were treated in the past (their original wounding) has an influence over how they treat themselves in the present, how they treat people around them, and how they respond to how they are treated by others. A bit of a mouthful I know, but stop and read it again.

To reinvent your life and make your relationships happier and more productive, all four levels need attending to.

This secret is the biggest secret of self-awareness. It's called **the formula**, and it goes like this:

Secret number 16: Whatever was done to you originally, you still expect it to be done to you, you do it to yourself, and you do it to others.

It sounds simple, and once you know how to work the formula, healing can also be simple. Transformation needn't be a complicated thing. What it needs to be is effective, successful, and lasting.

Your past affects your present, and what happens in the present, shapes your future.

You learn about yourself more quickly by being in a relationship, than you do by being alone. Other people mirror back to you your image, your words, and your behaviours, often with lightning speed. It helps to not be in a full suit of armour when they do, so that you are more able to graciously accept their gift. If you are a highly evolved conscious creature, with a lot of self-development and awareness behind you, and you really like and respect who you are and how you behave, then you probably won't have a problem with seeing your reflection. If your reflection makes you run for the hills, or if you are just happy to keep evolving, read on.

For change to be effective and long lasting, it's helpful to comprehend how all four levels of the formula might affect you. If you only seek to understand one level, the other three could trip you up at some point and limit your ability to transform. When you make changes to all four levels you can expect these things to occur:

1. Being open, curious, and possibly forgiving towards the original wound means you can increase compassion for yourself and towards others. You may also gain an appreciation for the positive qualities you possess which more than likely came into play because of the original incident.
2. Being aware and able to recognize what belongs to you, what belongs to others, and being able to discern, release fear, reduce anger and any hyper-vigilance that occurs while you are expecting terrible stuff to happen, means you can regain the ability to calmly look through clear lenses in the present.
3. Making sense of your self-talk, self-care, self-esteem, and being more conscious of how self-respecting your choices towards yourself are, may propel you forward in a positive way.

4. Recognizing how your words, actions, and behaviours impact on the lives of others may increase your ability to be clear, caring, and respectfully attentive, which in turn promotes a greater reward; ease in your relationships with others.

Most change techniques tap into the universal desire to be happy, rather than encouraging you to accept the reality that things are also at times just downright difficult and could do with being appreciated, so they can then be transformed.

Dragons don't appear very often in tales, but when they do you can guarantee mishaps will follow. Their sheer size, along with their ability to breathe fire and sometimes fly, makes them a force to be reckoned with. Amidst the confusion of working out whether to seal the entrance to their den, or befriend them and hope for kindness in return, somewhere along the way if you just show courage, you will be rewarded.

Learning to accept difficulties, finding courage to understand more about those difficulties, and welcoming how they have shaped you, can enable you to live in a way where you get to see and greet the present moment with fresh eyes and untainted responses.

In fairytales and real life, people with no experience of appalling people, painful encounters, or seemingly insurmountable obstacles simply do not exist. Maybe they live in cartoons?

Here's how it goes. The more something was done to you originally, the more ingrained the pattern is likely to be in your life. In general, it's usually easier to blame, than it is to take responsibility and recognize that you may continue the pattern. (If you experienced abuse, you are completely entitled to blame!)

Let's look at an example from a case study, so you can better understand how the formula works:

Kim was nearly two when her parents separated. Her father was an alcoholic.

She can clearly identify her original wound. She felt abandoned. Firstly by her father leaving, and then many times after that when visits and trips away with her drunken father became inconsistent, danger-filled, and disappointing. She wanted an authentic emotional connection, yet rarely received one.

Consequently, Kim grew up expecting to be abandoned by friends and boyfriends. When some of them did eventually tire of her and dump her, she found it extremely difficult to use words to express herself, mostly because she was in the pre-verbal stage when the original abandonment occurred. In therapy when Kim experienced sadness, she would often raise her fingers to her mouth seemingly holding her words back. She would look down rather than make eye contact, and tap her fingers instead of saying what she needed to say. She, on occasion expected me to tire of her, give up, and terminate therapy. She had a tendency to mumble. She presented as negative and untrusting a lot of the time. This unconsciously contributed to many people avoiding her company; making her fears a reality.

How Kim treated herself was interesting. She used drugs to numb her pain and although she couldn't stand people who got drunk, she chose to not recognize that her addiction had the same potential to invite similar consequences as her father's. The lack of motivation and apathy that resulted from her nearly daily use of drugs was making her abandon her dreams in regards to her work and her passions. One day would roll into the next. She would feel bad that she wasn't achieving so she would get high to make herself feel better, and then feel bad again, and so the cycle would continue.

Kim wasn't able to express herself in a drugged state and as a result she constantly let her boyfriend down by promising to do something, or be somewhere. She frequently told him she couldn't understand why he would want to be with her. By year two in their relationship, she was clearly not there for him emotionally, her drug use was affecting things sexually, and she was acting in many ways that made him feel abandoned by her.

Level one for Kim was the easiest to identify. She disliked her father and blamed him for her troubles. Level two was also easy, and she went to great lengths to provide evidence that people weren't to be trusted. She had a list of abandonment stories as long as her arm to prove it. Level three and four were the most difficult for Kim. She couldn't see that she was doing exactly the same thing to herself and to others, that she had had done to her. Somehow she rationalized that it was okay to have been hurt, but she had a lot of trouble recognizing that she had the power to hurt herself and others. Recognizing that her boyfriend had taken on entirely similar feelings now to what she had experienced growing up with her absent father, was a shocking awakening and thankfully one that helped her get on the right track.

Exploring each level brought wisdom and relief for Kim. She even came to have more respect for her mother when she compassionately realized that her mother's choice to raise Kim by herself without her husband was a self-respecting, protective act. She learnt that disliking her father, and choosing to not see any of his good qualities, transferred into self-loathing. Kim came to see that her behaviours had clear consequences. She became conscious of the ways she actually invited others to abandon her. She did so through her tone, her choice of words and her lack of self-respect. Learning about addiction helped her understand that it is a genetically predisposed disease, and that her father had inherited similar wounds to herself, but unlike Kim, her father had never chosen to seek help.

This made Kim feel sad for her father, inviting a compassionate viewpoint for the first time in her life. By participating in treatment for addiction and remaining healthy, Kim had more energy and vitality and had a much better relationship with herself. She expressed herself more clearly, and made great inroads to being present and connected with her boyfriend. She grew to be consistent, trustworthy, positive, self-responsible, and able to love herself and others, which is clearly a great result.

It's important to remember that there is no standard method that covers how anyone chooses to respond to whatever happened to him or her originally. Wounds hold people captive in different ways. Five children, with the same kind of father as Kim, will more than likely have five different experiences, and five different explanations, as to how their father's behaviour affected them. For Kim she felt abandoned. Someone else could have chosen to idolize their father and blame their mother, or they could've decided to feel powerless from not being able to change their father. They may have believed that they themselves were bad and wrong and deserved to be neglected. Another person might've even welcomed the freedom that they experienced by not having a father around. Most people will believe that what happened to them was real, because their truth is their invention.

We are creative humans. Things happen, but what we *choose* to believe about what happens, is the thing to look at. Belief systems shape us. It's not about making what happened right or wrong. It's not about blaming parents or caregivers. It's about understanding our responses to the past, being clear about which choices we made, why we made them, and how those choices affect us in the present.

One level of the formula is usually easier to identify. It's likely that one will be glaringly obvious to you, but it is possible that it may only be obvious to others. It's not uncommon for the other levels to need some landmine sweeping or cave excavations to uncover them. The obvious one is usually the one that you may have already worked on in therapy or change workshops with some success, or it's the one your beloved will tend to point out to you over and over, or it will have something to do with *that* thing that you do that people complain about the most.

Understanding each level and how it infiltrates your thinking, feeling, and behaviour is the first step towards changing ingrained patterns and belief systems for good. Needless to say, even when someone thinks they have all four levels handled, there will always be more discoveries, as life is full of interesting surprises, mythical creatures, and dragon slayers.

Some people insist they have never had anything bad ever happen to them growing up. If this is familiar to you, maybe when you work the formula it could look a little like this:

Level one:

What was done to you was that everything was done right, with lots of love and attention.

Level two:

You could still expect that things are done right, with lots of love and attention, so look out when you hit the real world of relationships and hook up with someone with emotional baggage, which is close to ninety percent of the planet. That's when you suddenly might not know what to do or where to begin dealing with the difficulty in front of you.

Level three:

You probably take very good care of yourself so it's possible that those around you may find that hard to compete with, understand, or keep up with.

Level four:

Your expectations in regards to how others behave, or treat you, may be unreasonable, or unreachable.

You don't even need a dragon to show up at your door and hold you captive to expose a calamity. It would be near impossible for anyone to not be affected in some way by the mishaps and misfortune of what happens out there in the world. Things like financial downturns, climate disasters, war, famine, suffering (both natural and manmade) can affect you, make you wonder, increase discernment, and hopefully make you want to outwit, protect, show kindness, sacrifice, or save in some way.

Go ahead and:

- explore what your original wound was;
- take time-out with paper and a pen;
- do the exercise with a trusted friend; or
- if you think it's going to be really difficult, book a therapy session to help determine your answers and get support to guide you through unexplored terrain.

Like symbolism in fairytales, your unconscious is a window to another world worth adventuring to.

"Perhaps the dragons in our lives are princesses who are only waiting to see us act, just once, with beauty and courage. Perhaps everything that frightens us is, in its deepest essence, something helpless that wants our love."
Rainer Maria Rilke.

Here is a chart to help trigger you and get you thinking:

Behaviour you may display that is dysfunctional:	What might have happened to you in the past:	How it could have affected you:	What you need to aim for in order to heal:
Fanatical or socially disconnected	Strong or negative influences forced upon you. No room for your identity. Abuse.	Who am I? How do I fit in? You may seek to belong to a gang or group that isn't socially acceptable. You may feel shame.	Find your own identity and direction. Be yourself. Share yourself. Learn how to be flexible and reasonable.
Needy, or a cold loner	Love withheld. Neglect. Not enough healthy bonding. Abandonment.	Has difficulty giving and receiving love. May have an unrealistic or unhealthy regard for others.	Be willing to open up. Learn to give and take in a healthy balanced way. Be considerate to others.
Busy-body or a disinterested cynic	Rejection. Abandonment. Lack of appropriate care.	You may waste your energy and have difficultly being productive and self-caring.	Find a good use for your time and energy. Give to yourself. Propel yourself forward and contribute in a healthy way.

Arrogant or blaming	Unwise attitudes passed on. Emotional detachment. Lack of spiritual guidance. Victimized.	You may display intolerance and be difficult to get close to. You could struggle to accept others' viewpoints and struggle to find a deeper meaning and purpose to life.	Take responsibility for your own direction. Celebrate achievements. Recognize wisdom. Form healthy balanced friendships. Be calm.
Withdrawn or neurotic	Abuse. Not being comforted or cared for in an appropriate way. Being in danger.	Difficulty trusting and having faith. Could carry a belief that you punish or will be punished.	Have hope and believe that most people are safe. Trust that life will work out. Find inner strength and internal security.
Impulsive or compulsive	Being shamed. Not enough belief that you are capable.	Could have a problem with willpower and self-control. Prone to addiction. Lack of judgement.	Be independent and responsible. Create safety and boundaries. Learn to hold on and let go.

Boring or thoughtless	Made to feel guilty. Not enough exploration and play. Overprotected.	May have difficulty fitting in. Finds it hard to make decisions and be creative.	Be courageous. Find a purpose and direction. Play. Take appropriate risks.
Obsessive or lacking in purpose	Made to feel inferior or incompetent. Not valued. Addiction.	Difficulty believing in yourself. May find it difficult to learn.	Be productive. Feel a sense of achievement and accomplishment. Aim for realistic results.

To investigate level one, answer these questions:

Name what you think was done to you.

- Who did it?
- How often did he or she do it?
- Why do you believe they did it?
- What effect did it have on you?
- What harm was done?
- What do you believe to be true about yourself because of it?
- What do you believe about life because of it?
- What do you feel angry about?
- What do you wish he or she could have done differently?
- What did you long for that never seemed to happen?
- What specific things could have been done better in childhood?
- Why would you like to heal it?
- How would you feel if it was healed?

Once you have some clarity around your original wound, then it's time to take the next step and work out which lenses you choose to look through at the world, and how you choose to view the people in front of you. This one may take some imagination and exploration.

To investigate level two, answer these questions:

Name what you think is going to be done to you.

- Who might do it?
- Why do you think he or she will?
- What is it about them that will make them do it?
- When do you think he or she will do it?
- How might you end up feeling when they do it?
- What might you feel after they do it?
- Who actually does it?
- How often do they do it?
- Why do you believe they do it?
- What is it about you that could make them want to do it?
- What effect does it have on you?
- What harm is being done?
- What do you believe to be true about yourself when it happens?
- What do you believe about them when they do it?
- What do you feel angry about?
- What do you wish they could do differently?
- What do you wish you could do differently?
- What do you long for that he or she isn't doing?
- What specific things could be done better?
- Why would you like to heal it?
- How do you think you would feel if it was healed?
- How do you think you can stop it occurring?
- What could you do differently to break the pattern?
- What could you ask them to do to help you break the pattern?

Now you have identified your original wound, and you have an idea of what you expect to experience from others, it could be time to look at how these two themes you have explored influence how you treat yourself.

Drop down into a quiet honest space and explore the next step.

To investigate level three, answer these questions:

Name what you do.

- How do you do it to yourself?
- How many ways does it manifest?
- Why do you do it?
- How often do you do it?
- What effect does it have on you?
- What harm are you doing?
- What might happen if you keep doing it?
- What do you believe to be true about yourself when you do it?
- What do you believe about life when you do it?
- What do you feel angry about?
- What do you wish you could do differently?
- What specific things could you do differently to make life ideal?
- Why would you like to heal it?
- How would you feel if you didn't do it anymore?

For some people the next step is often the hardest.

We hardly ever want to admit that we might be capable of behaving in ways that could be detrimental to others.

Just in case there is a possibility that it could be a teeny bit true, why not go ahead and investigate?

You may find just a few ways of being that could be tweaked. With abandonment for example, it may be that you tune out occasionally instead of being fully present and observant.

Keep digging!

For level four, answer these questions:

Name what you do to others.

- How do you do it to them?
- How many ways does it manifest?
- Why do you do it?
- How often do you do it?
- What effect does it have on you?
- What effect do you think it has on him or her?
- What harm might you be doing?
- What might happen if you keep doing it?
- What do you believe to be true about yourself when you do it?
- What do you believe about him or her, when you do it to them?
- What do you feel angry about?
- What do you wish you could do differently?
- What specific things could you do differently?
- Why would you like to heal it?
- How would you feel if you didn't do it anymore?

More questions you could answer to deepen your understanding:

- What could I do to avoid harm or harming?
- What would need to happen to stop it occurring?
- Why do I need to heal it?
- How can I heal it?
- Who can help me heal it?
- When can I do that?
- What kinds of help might I need?
- Where might I get that help?

For each of the four levels:

Invite compassion in.

- Did they, or you, know how to do it any differently at the time?
- What made them, or you, do what you did?
- Were they young? Addicted? Damaged?
- Did he or she know any better?
- If you knew better, do you think you would do better?

Depersonalise.

- Reduce emotion.
- Seek to understand why people do what they do.
- Affirm: How other people behave towards me often has nothing to do with me, and everything to do with them.
- Or affirm: How I behave towards others often has nothing to do with them, and everything to do with me.

Act out what you never got to say.

Imagine the person you want to resolve things with is sitting in a chair in front of you. They may be imaginary, but the process is real. Try to see him or her there, and feel your feelings. Express what you need to, really standing up for yourself in the process. Have your metaphoric sword, shield, or suit of armour ready if you think you might need it.

Imagine what your life could've looked and felt like, had it taken a different path. The outcome may look ideal, or it may not.

List three positive things that have occurred to you as a result of experiencing something less fortunate.

- Most experiences have a silver lining or some good that eventually comes out of them.
- Celebrate your strength and creativity.
- Remember amidst adversary, you can find a way to prevail.

List some of the ways that your painful experiences have made you stronger and better.

Think of some of the positive things that are present in you because of the difficulty you experienced. For example if you hadn't experienced loss so young, you wouldn't perhaps have so much empathy for others.

Offer forgiveness to those who hurt you, only if it's appropriate to do so, and forgive yourself.

Try doing Sharon Salzberg's amazingly healing Loving Kindness Meditation. http://www.oprah.com/spirit/Opening-the-Heart-Through-Lovingkindness-Meditation

Be creative.

- What could you symbolically do to hand an experience back to the person or people who hurt you?
- Choose an object to represent your good and less good experiences, and do something with them that releases their hold on you.
- Float flowers down a river, let wishes go in a balloon, or plant a tree to commemorate your ability to thrive.
- Jump from a confidence course on flying ropes and yell like a fearsome dragon if it helps.

Once you have a better grasp on how your past affects your present, and you understand why you do what you do, and you can clearly see why others do what they do, the next step is to stay alert to all of the feelings and behaviours you have discovered. It may take up to six months to get a really good grip on discerning which reactions and behaviours stem from your original wound, and which ones are just everyday emotional responses to present day happenings. Curiously sift and sort through them all. Knowing the difference will help your relationships profoundly. It takes observation and application to begin to ignore, transform, and enforce good self-talk and to reach for new responses, behaviours, and communication that serve you and others better.

Welcome the idea that change is possible at any moment.

Find peace with the past strength in the present and hope for the future.

Part TWO

Aiming for 'Just Right'

This second part, *Aiming for 'Just Right'* is about seeing, strengthening, and making the best of what you have. It's about:

- communicating in ways that bring you more comfort;
- getting to the emotional heart of what really matters;
- learning to be understood; and
- gaining a deeper understanding of the roles you and your beloved play.

Focusing on an outcome you do want, and positively moving in that direction knowing you have a workable combination (which may only require a bit of moderate shaping rather than any extreme changes to make it just right) is not an impossible task.

Let's trust you have the right partner, one that's not too soft or too hard. Hopefully unlike *Goldilocks*, you didn't bust into someone else's house to find them. Let's imagine, and keep imagining that your beloved is enticing, delectable, and they fulfil your once upon a dream, forever and always. Now you can work on creating a really safe haven to house your love in.

When we are accessible, responsive, respectful, and are expectant of the same in return, our connections continue to grow stronger and last the distance.

Secret number 17: Creating longevity is about understanding differences, being respectful, and remembering to recognize positive qualities.

Now's the time to find and gather up, all of the positive benefits of being together, and acknowledge the effort that you and your beloved have put in. It's about being willing to spot strengths and celebrate what's right, rather than concentrating on what's not right. It's about encouraging useful attitudes and behaviours, communicating consciously and effectively, and discussing all things in reasonable ways.

Aiming for 'Just Right' is about looking at the raw workings, the coming together of the two of you and finding ways to share a lifetime of love that stays secure and dependable; where you like, love, have compassion, and confide in each other. It's a resourceful reminder to constantly build your friendship and togetherness, authentically and safely, on solid foundations.

Your foundations need to be as solid as possible to:

- accommodate diverse interests;
- account for different tastes;
- tolerate varying temperatures of porridge, size of chairs, and softness of bed; and
- enable you to harmoniously co-exist under one roof.

This is the time to learn how to make your footings and foundations sturdier, to look at what works, what doesn't, and figure out what you might need more of.

The most brilliant way to construct a grand castle is to have:

- a good set of plans;
- clear instructions;
- teamwork;
- guidelines that specify safety and appropriateness;
- insulation to add warmth;
- comforting finishing touches;
- no wandering bears; and definitely
- no hooligans or vandals.

Make sure your construction is substantial enough to survive:

- any destructive elements that could hurtle your way;
- the arrival of huffing and puffing wolves; and
- further additions at a later date.

So, let's go ahead and cement in qualities that celebrate permanence and durability. Get your hard hat on, conjure up joy and determination, and get ready to learn about the kind of self-control in the following pages that can enable you to respond to others clearly, compassionately, and from a position of personal power.

Try to not scrunch your nose up at trying new things. Give them a go. Three goes if you have too, until it feels just right.

The Princess and the Pea

The Princess and the Pea is a tale about a prince who experienced some difficulty trying to find a suitable princess to marry. Something always felt intuitively wrong with all the ones he met. He also couldn't be certain they were real princesses. One stormy night, a rain-drenched, bedraggled young woman sought shelter in the prince's castle. She claimed to be a princess, but the prince's mother was unsure and decided to test their guest by placing a pea under twenty mattresses in the bed she was to sleep in. When the princess awoke she was asked how she slept. She was honest and told them that she endured a sleepless night; kept awake by something hard in the bed which she was certain had bruised her. The prince was overjoyed with her expression of honesty, because only a real princess would have the sensitivity to feel a pea through twenty mattresses. The two married and lived happily ever after, and the pea was placed in the Royal Museum.

Now that you have mastered *Nurturing the Princess Within,* you may:

- appreciate and recognize the importance of knowing yourself thoroughly;
- have made great inroads into understanding why you are the way you are;
- feel more comfortable in your own skin; and
- be ready to learn how to happily merge your life with your beloveds.

Just like the princess in the *Princess and the Pea,* it pays to be a polite, authentic truth-speaker. Her confidence to seek shelter from the storm, and her ability to calmly and honestly speak up about her little irritant (the pea) threw the course of her life onto an exciting love-filled path. Sometimes we just need to trust that things happen for good reasons, even if they grate us at the time.

The prince was someone who fully trusted his inner voice. His intuition led him to pay attention to the knock on his door and he displayed a willingness to wait because he wanted to be with someone he belonged with, someone that fulfilled his need for an equal. Let's face it; this tale has a number of points that prove there's a silver lining in a storm cloud. If he weren't so difficult to please, if he had just gone and settled for any one of the other girls he dated, if he didn't wait for his true love, then he wouldn't have found happiness with the drenched princess. Surely because of his patience and sacrifice, she will view the relationship as an awesome privilege. That's a love worth maintaining!

There will always be a few obstacles along the way. Whose mother in law doesn't overly check the credentials of a possible daughter in law? Luckily the princess didn't once feel she had to prove herself. Even in a dishevelled state she waited for them to get to know her. She knew she was good enough, and when you know you are good enough, it's just a matter of time and patience before recognition, acknowledgement, and rewards come.

Now, I'm not suggesting you put any vegetables in the bed to test the validity of your partnership.

What I do suggest is this:

- Practise patience.
- Be your true self.
- Know that you are good enough.
- Hold out for what you believe in.
- Never settle for less than you deserve.
- Hold out for goodness.
- Be mindful.
- Listen to your intuition.
- Listen to the wisdom of others.
- Be assertive.
- Embrace vulnerability.
- Don't get too irritated if things don't go your way.
- Trust the process.
- Remember that small things can make a very big difference.

Focus on goodness and be hopeful.

How to Turn Straw into Gold

Rumpelstiltskin is a rags to riches fairytale in which a poverty-stricken miller man greedily sacrifices his daughter to a king in a botched investment scheme. An evil goblin who happens to be waiting in the wings, goes straight for the weakest point in the daughter, on one hand saving her from an impossible task of spinning straw into gold, and on the other hand making her offer the life of her first born in return for his favour. Fearful of the king (a bully who only gives her three days to spin the gold or she dies) she agrees. The evil goblin returns after the king makes the girl his queen, and gives her three days to guess his name or he will take the child. Unluckily for him, she is resourceful enough to send a messenger out into the world that makes a lot of successful enquiries. When the girl tells him she knows his name, *Rumpelstiltskin* becomes incensed, stamps his foot, and splits himself in two.

The *Rumpelstiltskin* tale is yet another reminder to be authentic, to consider the consequences of our actions, to be careful what we agree to, and to give what we promise to give. It encourages resourcefulness and reinforces why enlisting help from experts is so important, especially in tricky negotiations. One of the morals of the tale is that we cannot banish problems that plague us, until we know what the name of the problem is. Perhaps the biggest unnamed problem that failing relationships anywhere in the world face, is a lack of respect. In marriage and civil unions, not many people want to use the word obey in their vows, but they usually agree to honour, because that is not such an impossible task. Honour, love, and respect are all intertwined. If we treat others with the same amount of respect that we would like to receive, then happiness will find us. There's a very good reason why one of life's laws is to do unto others, as you would have them do unto you.

Secret number 18: Before you communicate, put your brain into gear and consciously consider asking yourself this: If I say this, in this way, then what is the likely result?

The miller man was so busy talking up his greatness and being inauthentic, spinning what he believed to be a good yarn to the king, that he was totally unconscious as to *what* he was saying, *how* he was saying it (boastfully) or the reason *why* (to impress) and look what happened, he had to hand his daughter over or be proven a liar. Why do people feel the need to over inflate themselves and why does it often seem easier for people to be pleasant or more tolerant to strangers, than those closest to them? As nice as it is to generously bestow respectful conversation upon a king, stranger, friend, or colleague, it's even better to be polite and authentic to the ones we love. It's an amazing feat to be able to think about what you say before you say it, and it's very self-caring to have some awareness of the possible outcome.

Secret number 19: It's always about what you say, how you say it, and the intention behind it.

Good, conscious, respect-filled communication creates safety, trust, and dependability. Respect creates a positive environment where friendship grows.

This tale also reminds us that apart from clear communication, the best way to riches (or proper ways to turn straw into gold) financially or emotionally, is creative, consistent hard work. Long lasting love doesn't have too many shortcuts, and nor should it. The basics just need honouring. We all want to be loved and accepted, and despite how most of us behave, we want it to be easy. We want those who love us, to notice our good traits and recognize our potential, and we definitely don't want to be tossed aside or traded in for the next best thing.

Secret number 20: Love, simply because you can, and because others deserve to be loved.

The evil goblin offered help, a seemingly loving act, but it was really just a greedy act in disguise. Real love is never selfish. Real love is about giving and doing, and less about getting. It's not about desperation, grasping, or expecting a particular thing in return. Love is not reliant upon the other person changing to suit us, although that is what the majority of couples seeking couple's therapy expect will occur. They generally want to focus on what's *not* working, find out whose fault it is, and then fix it.

The way to a positive outcome is to actually focus on things that *are* working. Look at what's right with what you already have, and then improve it by being more positive, supportive, and full of praise. Manage your own responses and behaviours. Expect and accept positive behaviours from your beloved while individually rediscovering your wants, needs, and passions. The rewards you receive from doing this will further encourage you to know that what you are doing is working. Being conscious, attentive, and interested, improves listening skills and reduces stress. Letting go of bitterness and regret and refusing to waste energy on what ifs and maybes, leads to more contentment.

Let's look at a case study to highlight how positive change can occur:

James was polite to his staff and customers, yet talked to his wife as if she were a naughty puppy. He snapped at her in a sharp tone and expected her to fulfil his requests at a moment's notice despite her own busy schedule, and he had no hesitation barking orders at her in front of other people. A little part of James was like the miller man in that he didn't appreciate or value her enough. Julie said it was like living with Dr Jekyll and Mr Hyde. She didn't know when he would snap next, and she came to therapy physically and emotionally withdrawn, wanting to make exit strategies. Her nerves were frayed and she had given up seeing any good in James whatsoever. She looked a little like she had been locked in a tower with straw for a companion for a good few months! Julie was confused because she could see he was capable of respectful communication, and hurt because she believed he obviously didn't care about her enough to speak to her in a respectful way. She had taken up sleeping in the spare room and flinched at the thought of becoming intimate with him again. She didn't think he deserved it, much like the king didn't deserve to gain an instant wife who didn't have any say in the matter. James said he felt unloved by Julies' withdrawal. He believed that she was the problem and said that she was on her way out of the marriage, so he couldn't be bothered investing positive energy into their communication. He said his attitude changed when he felt powerless to fix something that was obviously broken.

Rather than focusing on why the dynamic was in place, Julie was asked to put aside her resentment and try a few new things:

1. Ask to be talked to with respect every time she wasn't.
2. Clarify her boundaries, and feel deserving.
3. Reconnect with James and act as though she liked him again, despite her reaction to recoil at the very thought of being kind to him.
4. To stop behaving as though he were *Rumpelstiltskin.*

Julie was very visual, so it was helpful for her to pretend to look through new lenses at James. She began to tell him more frequently what she appreciated about him, and made herself touch him again, bringing back the gentleness and caring that she had been neglecting.

James's reaction was actually incredibly speedy, mostly due to Julie moving back into their shared bed. He began calling her nice names again and took time using a full sentence to ask her for what he needed, rather than being demanding. James was asked to see the relationship as a vessel without a crack in it. It was important that he view their relationship as something worth investing in, just like it was worth talking to staff politely in order to keep them in the job. He was encouraged to find as many ways as possible to not burst open the crack, and he was grateful for the promise of more intimacy returning if he could do that.

Both Julie and James made a list of what they were originally attracted to in each other, and promised to behave more like best friends, except with the addition of sex.

They each had a signal:

Julie's was to put her hand up and say, "How about you try that again nicely, in a way that I will respond positively to."

James's was to smile and flutter his eyelashes and say, "Please sweetheart," before any order he gave to her, even at work.

Taking away the sharp edges certainly did the trick. They found softness, resolution, renewed respect and closeness, and hopefully, you know, they lived happily ever after!

If you have difficulty waiting for someone to make the first move, could it be time to give up being stubborn? Stalemate situations have a horrible tendency to cause erosion. Why not exhibit willingness, and be the one to make a positive difference?

Moving forward with gentleness, humour, and respect always works so much better.

Dark Caves and Deep Woods

"The cave you fear to enter holds the treasure you seek."
Joseph Campbell.

Visiting our shadow side and facing our fears, the hidden parts of ourselves we sometimes refuse to recognize in the light of day, often requires us to become cave explorers, donning a hardhat and flashlight and going about the business of bravely discovering the darker places of the soul.

The uncertainty of self-discovery can be scary. It's understandable to experience fear and anxiety, but it's also good to remember that fear sits very close to excitement. In fairytales, caves house the odd dangerous thing. On any journey into the unknown we could stumble across a troll guarding treasure in a cave, or we could come face to face with a fierce bear protecting her cubs. It's helpful to be prepared for surprises, to breathe through any fear that surfaces, to relish the excitement and stimulation, and to know that going within eventually offers protection and shelter.

Secret number 21: A shadow is just a shadow, and shadows needn't hold any threats.

Shadows are that which we think we are not.

Invite shady, hidden parts (like selfish, greedy, angry parts) out of forgotten corners. Encourage unresolved conflicts, suppressed traumas, rage, and any supposedly shameful or guilty stuff out of the darkness. Bring them all out into the light, and integrate them into the rich mix of all of who you are.

The Uses Of Enchantment: The Meaning and Importance of Fairy Tales by Bruno Bettelheim talks about how important deep woods are in fairytales, especially in the tale "The Two Brothers" where two brothers go into a forest, take counsel with each other, and come to an agreement. The forest they enter, he says, "Symbolizes the place in which inner darkness is confronted and worked through; where uncertainty is resolved about who one is; and where one begins to understand who one wants to be." Bettelheim goes on to say: "Since ancient times the near impenetrable forest in which we get lost has symbolized the dark, hidden, near-impenetrable world of our unconscious. If we have lost the framework which gave structure to our past life and must now find our way to become ourselves, and have entered this wilderness with an as yet undeveloped personality, when we succeed in finding our way out we shall emerge with a much more highly developed humanity."

Secret number 22: Sometimes renovation needs to occur outside of your relationship, in order to make you more present and less distracted inside your relationship.

Struggling with unresolved pain from our past is another hurdle likely to affect our ability to be fully aware and consciously available in our daily interactions. Not being present can dull sensitivity, to the self and towards others. It can separate us from being able to receive love, affection, and attention from others. It can also make us unavailable to give love, affection, and attention. Figuratively it can put us in a dark cave or deep woods, a place where others don't feel they can venture into. If you often feel overwhelmed or triggered by certain things, it's possible that something from your past is hanging around in the shadows. Dig deeper into your past if you find yourself:

- finding fault;
- blaming;
- using words that aren't warranted;
- having moods that don't fully correspond to the situation you are in;
- picking unnecessary fights;
- acting out behaviours that sometimes appear to be inappropriate;
- having reactions that feel way bigger than you would like them to be;
- producing responses that invite devastation and destruction;
- surrounded by memories that eat you up; or you feel
- distant, troubled, and preoccupied.

Acknowledging and attending to uncomfortable truths from your past can clear a path forward. Things that hold you back needn't be dramatic or secretive.

Maybe someone from your past behaved in way that made you:

- feel bad about yourself;
- question your self-worth; or
- distrust yourself and others.

If that gets in your way now, maybe it could do with being challenged.

Step into your own light and shine brightly.

- Believe in your talent.
- Recognize your needs.
- Do whatever it takes to make your brilliance noticed.
- Stand up and be worthy, deserving, and proud.
- Communicate how you feel, what you think, and express what's going on for you.

What if your pain was enormous? If you suffered some kind of abuse in the past and carry an unshared secret, know that it's never too late to hope for, or create a peace-filled reality. Perhaps you struggle to make good choices? Or maybe you feel resilient and strong, simply from surviving your experience? Hiding memories away in a deep dark cave doesn't always stop them from affecting you. What's important is to work out whether your way of coping is functioning as fabulously as it could.

Secret number 23: Many times people who try to shut out pain, lock pleasure out with it.

If we disconnect and numb ourselves to avoid feeling, not only do we shut out pain, we shut out pleasure. The more pain we clear through, and the more we allow ourselves to feel, the less scary it becomes. The more you do it, the easier it gets. Releasing the past can help restore control and bring more joy. Most of the time there is no pain that we cannot survive. Sometimes we just need to surrender into accepting love and expert support to get us through extra tough times. Just know that when you break things down into bite size pieces, they become more manageable.

What if the person who troubles you is a stranger, is dead, or is extremely difficult to communicate with? Many people are unsafe to be around, incapable of hearing feelings, and are unsympathetic to the needs of others. Even if they are likely to cause you physical danger or are just plain unreachable, don't give up.

Realistically, releasing and expressing still works without having to personally confront someone. You could use another method like letter writing. Have it be okay to book a therapy session and allow an expert to guide you in your recovery. However you do it, just find a safe way to get it all out.

How to search more deeply:

- List the consequences that their problem has, or has had on you.
- Include how it affected your spiritual, emotional, physical, sexual, social, and financial parts of you.
- Say how his or her behaviour makes you feel and behave now.
- List things you want to let go of, such as covering up, making excuses, feeling closed off, being shy, feeling aggressive, not trusting, being preoccupied, having control issues, or blaming.
- Remain open to your feelings as you write.
- Know that if you have been hiding in a cave for a long time, coming out can feel extremely vulnerable.

When you have a breakthrough, celebrate your courage and coping strategies.

Fear of rejection and the challenges that can arise when confronting others, often stops people from telling the truth. Others may keep a secret because they are terrified of uncovering shame. Shame is when you believe you are inherently wrong or bad, which we know you aren't. Speak out. Do it anyway. Be vulnerable. As the fabulous highly skilled shame expert Dr. Brene Brown says, "Owning our story can be hard but not nearly as difficult as spending our lives running from it. Embracing our vulnerabilities is risky but not nearly as dangerous as giving up on love and belonging and joy - the experiences that make us the most vulnerable. Only when we are brave enough to explore the darkness will we discover the infinite power of our light."

Just keep taking baby steps; one stepping stone at a time, no matter how dark the woods are, into eventual sunshine.

- Scars are stronger than skin.
- Healing is always possible.
- Your needs, feelings, wants, and your healing are worth bringing to life.

Secret number 24: Whenever you decide to disclose something, it's important to be realistic about the responses you might encounter.

Unfortunately there is never any guarantee that you will be fully heard or understood when you choose to bring important things to light. You may also never get the outcome you desire. Whatever happens, remember these three things:

1. Be realistic.
2. Know that mayhem may strike at any time.
3. Preparation is everything.

Even when you are able to tell the truth and say how someone else's behaviour affects you, doesn't mean you can change that person, or control the outcome any more than you could have in the past. Whatever they have done, or are doing, or however they feel about you and your choices, is probably pretty ingrained and integrated into his or her entire way of being. The very least you can do is bring it to their attention and see what happens. These examples show how varied the consequences can be. Those who pluck up the courage to tell important people in their lives that they are gay can experience results ranging from being ostracized to being loved even more. Adopted people seeking to reconnect with their birth parents, can have results ranging from being welcomed with open arms and floods of happy tears into a new family, to having their existence continue to be denied. Sometimes nothing goes the way you expect.

The result however, is not why you need to disclose, and a perfect result is not what you ought to strive for. It's the expression of your truth, the ability to be honest with yourself and those close to you that's important. Have hope. Find courage. Stand in your truth. Whatever the subject matter, know that whenever you release things that block you, you move into being the open, engaged person you know you can be. That can bring satisfaction and empowerment.

Secret number 25: When you begin to understand all the parts of yourself, your shadow self and your conscious self, then you can open a chest filled with treasure.

As Howard Sasportas an important voice in contemporary astrology once said, "Denial is pushing something out of your awareness. Anything you hide in the basement has a way of burrowing under the house and showing up on the front lawn."

Doesn't that saying just conjure up such a great image? Understanding all parts of yourself means going into the dark side, looking at whatever issues you repress, deny, disown, or despise. They are the culprits that make their way to the surface and cause extremes. (And mounds of dirt!)

Isn't it interesting how many:

- alcoholics insist they don't really have a problem with drinking;
- strait-laced people can secretly have unsafe sex;
- overly-moral and righteous people can do others wrong;
- penny-pinching people can gamble;
- sugary-sweet people can lie and cheat;
- highly principled people can be cruel in their private world?

Aggressive, sexual, and addictive secrets tend to lurk around in the shadows. Ignored, rejected, repressed and clandestine subjects have a tendency to force people to behave in destructive and sneaky ways. When covert things rise to the surface in a big way and get exposed, people can act as though the devil made them do it. Or, they end up in a scandal so enormous in scale, that it becomes difficult to explain or understand. It's a fast way to end up splattered all over the media, landing oneself fair and square in a pot of boiling water, or behind bars.

What can be done to bring the shadow self into the light of day?

- Recognize it's a problem and be honest about its existence.

Leanne French

- Take ownership, embrace and accept the difficulty.
- Take responsibility for your actions.
- Ask how the shadow helps or hinders you in your average day.
- Be curious as to what purpose the shadow thinks it's serving.
- Make amends where harm has been caused.
- Aim to express yourself truthfully.
- Forgive yourself and get appropriate help.
- Find a positive outlet to express this part of you or what it represents.

When we investigate each part we are made of, it becomes much easier to see whether the choices we are making are healthy ones. What can emerge from our willingness to go deeply into our core is a more comfortable, aware, and creative self. It can enable us to be more fully alert in the drivers' seat. Projecting judgements onto others becomes less likely. Owning what's going on in our unconscious can help us stay accountable for misplaced emotions.

Secret number 26: Discomfort helps you grow, so get comfortable with being uncomfortable.

One of the reasons why entering into therapy can bring up truth and discomfort so readily for people, is because it takes place in unfamiliar surroundings, with an unfamiliar person. The therapist's care, compassion, and intense focus on you can make it easier to find hidden treasure. When they focus on you, and you focus on yourself, it becomes more difficult to become distracted or sidetracked. In fairytales, it's akin to finding yourself alone in a dark cave or deep woods. Without distraction it's easier to see how you operate. It also enables concentrated exploration of outcomes, and generates possibilities. It pays to trust that no matter what happens, you always have the answers within. You can generally find your own way even if the birds decide to eat your trail of breadcrumbs!

Searching deeply and getting an honest appraisal helps:

- restore balance;
- enables you to recognize limits and set boundaries;
- invites clarity around what you can do and won't do; and
- encourages self-responsibility.

When you become comfortable with discomfort, it can bring more aliveness into your existence. You are more likely to welcome change, and more able to receive feedback. That is the moment when difficult material transforms into treasure in disguise, and the magic and wonder begins to unfold.

"The sad truth is that man's real life consists of a complex of inexorable opposites—day and night, birth and death, happiness and misery, good and evil. We are not even sure that one will prevail against the other, that good will overcome evil, or joy will defeat pain. Life is a battleground. It always has been, and always will be; and if it were not so, existence would come to an end."
Carl Jung.

Wild Imaginings

Fairytales parallel common human conditions. They resonate deep within us in an emotionally creative way and invite us into illogical, impractical, unrealistic, wonderful, and terrifying worlds where good opposes evil, magic exists, and animals transform into people. Somehow fairytales make us face the truth about ourselves, and what we identify with. They encourage us to touch in on, and consider our own character. How would we behave if faced with similar situations or choices? What would we do or say? The imaginary world of fairytales has a bunch of things in common with the real world. Tales reflect the inner world of our thoughts, and bring to our attention things that we all face in love relationships. In life, love, and fairytales there are adventures, risks, consequences, and outcomes that require careful consideration, calm choices, and oodles of creativity.

Wild imagination is a magnificent thing to have running around, except when conflict rears its ugly head. That's when it's important to grasp hold of anxiety, fear, and phobias and seek to transform them. Anger definitely needs cooling down, and fantasy has to be put aside. (It can easily be reawakened at a more convenient time.) If you're striving for clarity, it's better to reach for truth and a dose of reality.

Mindfulness is the one magical thing that effectively dampens conflict. Purposefully, attentively increasing present moment awareness helps us regulate emotion. Fine-tuning our focus brings us cleverly in touch with our thoughts and responses in a way that increases consciousness, especially around where we focus our attention, and why we do.

Practicing mindfulness meditation regularly ensures we recognize the difference between thoughts and feelings in ways that allow us to be present and responsible, rather than being reactive or oppositional. When you can distinguish reactivity, and realise you have many choices around what you feel and say and do in response to others, you can reduce stress and be more open to the many positive possibilities and avenues of expression available.

How to bring mindful resolution to relationship difficulties:

- Learn to let go.
- Reduce hyper-vigilance.
- Change the idea that situations have to be stressful.
- When situations unfold, see them as a challenge rather than a threat.
- Look through compassionate eyes.
- Remember that you and your beloved are partners on the same team, not opponents.

Secret number 27: Your partner's behaviour has nothing to do with you.

People just do what they do. How you respond to what they do is what matters. People that love you rarely set out to purposefully hurt or harm you. That's assuming of course that they aren't psychopaths, and in that case they don't actually love you, they just want to own you, and you shouldn't be with them. Always steer clear of *Bluebeard*!

Secret number 28: If what you are doing isn't working, stop and do it differently.

If you find yourself having very big emotional conversations inside your head as to why you are not loved enough, or not loved in the right way, just stop. It's that simple.

- Choose to not let any mindless monkey chatter rule you.
- Be here now.
- Change the channel.
- Reduce emotion.
- Aim for detachment.
- Breathe.
- Realise you have the power to change how you view any situation.
- Remember you have many other avenues of thought to choose from.
- Look for new possibilities and alternate avenues of expression.

Clearing away fog, fantasy, reactivity, and being present in times of emotional stress is a wise action plan. Staying emotionally intact, being mindful of your own thoughts rather than focusing on the behaviour of others is incredibly helpful.

Being mindful means you can choose which thoughts you keep in your head, and which words come out of your mouth.

Eight steps to follow to become more mindful:

1. Watch your thoughts come, and then watch them go; just like clouds floating across the sky.
2. Watch one cloud at a time, and tell yourself how interesting it is to observe that particular cloud.
3. Breathe and wait for the kinds of thoughts to come that you want to have hanging around.
4. If upsetting thoughts continue, just go back and focus again on your breathing.
5. Breathe in, and breathe out. Low and slow.
6. Take your attention out to the sounds you hear, and then take your focus back to your steady breath.
7. Be aware of your physical self.
8. Feel your back leaning against your chair, and feel your feet press against the ground as you slowly breathe in and out.

Wild imaginings often have a way of popping up and chattering mindlessly. Fantasies can be full of all kinds of messages that poke at you. Ignore the unhelpful ones. They are the ones that beg you to believe your beloved purposefully withholds affection, is selfish, and doesn't pay you the right kind of attention. None of those thoughts serve you, so you mustn't let them go into overdrive.

Thinking that they are doing *it* to you, whatever *it* is, can spiral you into negative thinking and encourage you to behave in ways that generally have less than positive consequences.

Negative thoughts and feelings are always a choice. You can invite them in like an old habit, or you can choose to change them. You could imagine all kinds of reasons as to why someone has a mood or behaviour that doesn't suit you. You could self-obsess and make it all about you. You could tell yourself they are doing *it* to hurt you because you aren't good enough, or because you don't deserve to be loved. It's much better to give up trying to control how a certain situation should or could be.

Instead:

- Go and make a sandwich.
- Play beautiful music and allow the lyrics to fill your head.
- Run a bubble bath.
- Take a break from chaos and drama.
- Go for a walk around the block.
- Stay connected, rather than disconnected from his or her love.
- Concentrate on yourself.
- Rather than obsessing about something or someone you can't control, give yourself attention and energy.

Don't pay attention to incoming junk mail such as:

- I haven't been told I'm loved in ages.
- They probably don't want to be with me.
- Maybe I'm too demanding?
- Maybe they like someone else?

Take a more empowering, curious standpoint:

- Why aren't they able to say they love me?
- Where might that have come from?
- Where might he or she have learnt that?
- Do they need to know how important it is for me to hear I am loved?

Acknowledge your thoughts and feelings and just let them be. Notice your thoughts and feelings but don't struggle with them.

Stay curious and see if your feelings have a name attached, like insecurity, or fear of loss. Then breathe and ask if your thoughts are useful or not. Pick a different path to go down, or distract yourself from less than helpful thoughts by doing something constructive for your own peace of mind. The thought may stay, but you can act any way you want. Once you have a handle on that, inner peace reigns.

Secret number 29: You cannot control the behaviour of someone else. What you can control are your thoughts and responses.

So much energy is wasted battling with thoughts. If we do it for long enough, it can become difficult to contain any anger that simmers beneath the surface. Give angry thoughts too much space and they could make you want to do battle for real.

Imagine. What if other people are simply doing what they are doing, because they are able to, because they can, because they always have? What if they seriously, honestly don't even understand what they are doing? What if he or she has no intention of it affecting anyone else? What if it has nothing to do with you?

Then imagine confronting him or her with your wild imaginings and blurting out that they are being unloving or mean. Have you ever done that, told someone off for doing such and such, and received a completely shocked reaction? Nine times out of ten if they are shocked by what you have said, it's generally because they are! We need to believe them, we need to listen to his or her truth and give them a chance.

The angst we wrestle with, often isn't even visible to other people. The only head it fills, is likely to be our own. Instead, we need to focus within and wisely change our own thoughts.

When we concentrate more fully on ourselves, and pay less attention to what others are doing or not doing, it melts our anguish.

Curiosity is one of the great keys of mindfulness.

Curiosity leads us to ask gentle enquiring questions in non-threatening, non-demanding, non-blaming ways.

If you want answers and still want his or her behaviour to change:

- get them to think about why they do what they do;
- where it possibly stems from;
- what effect it has on others; and
- what they might like to do to change it.

They may step forward and tell you, or they may not. Whatever happens, reduce expectation and stay as open and as curious as possible. It's called being the naïve enquirer.

The three most important things you need to know about mindfulness:

1. Everything in the past has already happened, and you have no control over it.
2. Anything that is yet to occur, you have no control over.
3. The only thing you can control and manage effectively is the present moment.

If your beloved becomes inquisitive enough to want to know how you are influenced by what they do, then take ownership and tell them gently.

Move away from:

- blaming;
- shaming;
- telling;
- teaching; or
- preaching to get him or her to change what they are doing.

Instead, just use this effective formula:

When you...
(Name the behaviour.)

I feel...
(Explain how you feel.)

What I need and want is...
(Be clear about what you would prefer.)

Are you able to do this? (Get a commitment.)

Aim for curiosity and surrender rather than pursuit and entitlement.

Bedtime Stories

"Perfect love is rare indeed, for to be a lover will require that you continually have the subtlety of the very wise, the flexibility of the child, the sensitivity of the artist, the understanding of the philosopher, the acceptance of the saint, the tolerance of the scholar and the fortitude of the certain."
Leo Buscaglia.

Bedtime is only meant for three things:

1. Stories.
2. Sleep.
3. And if you're a grown-up? Sex.

Having a good sex life undoubtedly adds strength to a relationship. Being physically intimate bonds lovers together as life partners. It's the only thing you get to do with each other that you don't get to do with anyone else, therefore it's super special, sensual, and sacred.

Fairytales don't usually go into overly intimate details of how to get down and dirty, hot and steamy. Usually it's left to our imagination. So, rather than delve into techniques, here are various emotional nuts and bolts to consider.

Secret number 30: Men need sex in order to feel loved, and women need to hear that they are loved, in order to have sex.

Both genders insist that it's true. Because a man is curious and likely to peek at these pages about SEX (especially when it's in capital letters and especially when you purposefully leave this page lying open.) Here is some advice for him. If he doesn't get to read about it, you will no doubt find a way to get the information to him. A bedtime story perhaps? Luckily, the recipe for sexual satisfaction doesn't require a complicated manual.

Men, regarding foreplay:

- You need to start earlier in the day or week, and tell your darling nice things. Things like how great she looks, why she is special to you, how beautiful her eyes are, why she is the only one you long for, lots of those kinds of things.
- Tell her she is gorgeous and capable.
- Celebrate small occasions.
- Remember big occasions.
- Buy little gifts.
- Encourage and support her.
- Share affection throughout the day. A hug or a long gaze at anytime of the day invites closeness.
- Pashing now and again warms things up a treat.

Women, what's called for is for you to initiate and entice:

- Promise to do wicked things, and then do them. Always follow through.
- Let him know how happy you are to have him in your life.
- Value his input.
- Acknowledge his uniqueness.
- Genuinely praise his abilities and qualities. It's easy to do once you get used to it.
- Be interested and involved in his life, his work, and his projects. Take a special interest in things he feels passionate about.
- Tell him what you value about him.
- Tell him you are proud of him.
- Make time to be fully present in his company.
- Connect and focus in on making his life more fulfilling, and you will be rewarded.

It's normal when encountering unusual amounts of stress from external influences like grief, loss, moving house, and job adjustments, for sex to alter in frequency or enthusiasm. Natural physical changes such as illness, pregnancy, hormonal changes, and ageing, fall under the same category. What helps? Compassion. Time. Affection. No pressure. Love. Understanding. Failing that, try a night in a hotel.

Sex is a physical form of communicating. If you aren't talking in respectful, loving, healthy ways, then it's almost guaranteed you won't experience a fulfilling sexual exchange. You have to know what you want, how you want it, why you want it, and be able to communicate this clearly and openly to each other. If there is an imbalance of power it can show up quickly in the bedroom. Someone will either want too much too often, not want any at all, or use sex as an asset to be traded, none of which is satisfying or advisable.

There are a lot of variants when it comes to sex:

- Do you have enough time?
- Do you make time?
- Are you a sex in the morning, or sex in the evening type?
- Are your horny times compatible?
- Are you willing to compromise?
- Do you use the majority of your energy on other pursuits?
- Are you willing to connect?
- Are you aware of your triggers if you are a survivor of sexual abuse?

Secret number 31: Emotional safety encourages closeness. Being sexually close helps build a dependable relationship.

There is comfort in being together in an environment of caring and empathy. The more comfortable you are with each other, the more fun you can have.

Things that can hinder closeness:

- Knowing what another person's emotional and physical needs are but not meeting them, which could send a message that you either don't care about them, or you don't want to make a difference.
- Having underlying fears and insecurities.
- Being angry and jealous.
- Using manipulative behaviour such as neglect and dependence.
- Getting into constant power struggles.
- Not honouring or respecting clear rules and boundaries.
- Constantly eroding trust.

- Having low self-esteem because not feeling good enough about yourself could cause you to have difficulty seeing how fabulous someone else actually is.
- Refusing to be emotionally intimate, and not revealing enough about your deeper self.
- Acting like roommates rather than lovers.
- Taking each other for granted.
- Focusing on faults.
- Feeling bored, and not doing anything to change that.
- Being in a constant state of exhaustion, and using being tired as an excuse to not connect.
- Fighting in bed.
- Arguing.
- Twisting what the other person says.
- Not being willing to compromise.
- Withholding sex as punishment.
- Watching television in bed. Consider taking the television out of the bedroom and using a television guide to consciously choose what you want to watch, in another room.
- Compulsive behaviours that draw your attention away from being fully present with each other, including excessive use of computer time, addiction to porn, gambling, gaming, alcohol, or drugs.

Secret number 32: Give your best energy to those who mean the most.

Try not to let work, children, and outside commitments zap all your liveliness.

Hold some energy aside to ensure you are available, loving, caring, attentive, and connected to the one you share your life with. Refuse to take them for granted. You owe it to him or her, and yourself, so protect your superb investment.

In fairytales dark princes and delicious princesses fight their way through thorn bushes to get to each other. You don't read about them staying at the office late! You needn't trample on furry woodland creatures speeding towards your desired reward, but remember to at least make an effort.

Staying in love is about doing things to fall in love all over again.

Lovemaking isn't going to always be in a fantastical setting, but why not aim for that now and again? Why not make love on a train, in the rain, or somewhere in Spain? Sex doesn't always have to be the wild swing off the chandeliers kind of sex that blows your mind and sets off fireworks, but I would encourage you to aspire for that at least once a month. Adventure, exploration, and creativity can help you achieve necessary naughtiness. Work out what clears the way for great sex, and do that. It might mean leaving the children with a babysitter, having a bath or massage to really relax, or sharing a great bottle of wine.

- Set the scene, play games, and arouse your sexual appetite.
- There is nothing wrong with a quickie, a roll in the hay, speedy afternoon delight, or a touch of carpet burn on the lounge floor.
- However you choose to do it, make it about wanting to be together.
- Make yourself emotionally available, and be willing to love and give generously.
- Remind yourself that your partner is a bonus in your life, not a right.

Secret number 33: Nothing brings sexy back quicker than feeling praised, special, valued, and adored.

- Invite closeness in.
- Feel sexy.
- Be sexy.
- Be enthusiastic and seductive.
- Find things that make you giggle.
- Let go of being concerned with technical sexual things.
- Have fun finding G spots and perfect positions.
- Laugh.
- Invite happiness into your heart.
- Inject fun into each day.
- Treasure each other without distraction and exhaustion.
- Have enough time apart to make reconnecting exciting.
- Be more mysterious.
- Make date night a priority.
- Go on dates where you try entirely new things.
- Take turns coming up with thrilling, adventurous, or spicy activities.

- Get off the couch.
- Turn off the television and computer and do something together.
- Get out of the house.
- Make your bedroom a tidy sanctuary, somewhere you can both surrender and relax in without being distracted.
- Clear your head of jobs that need doing.
- Make sure you have privacy.
- Get out of town and go to a perfect hideaway to spark your libido.
- Partake of treats and indulgences.
- Remember it's all about scent, seduction, sincerity, spontaneity, surrender, and sensuality.
- Make an effort to please.
- Expect and want your connection to be a pleasurable experience.
- Use light and lingering contact.
- Kiss.
- Really kiss, pashing increases passion and body temperature and puts you quickly in the mood for more.
- Stimulate imagination.
- Invite curiosity.
- Show warmth.
- Be affectionate.
- Express gratitude.
- Try new things together.
- Get messy and have it be okay to be noisy.
- Make foreplay interesting.
- Create meaningful rituals like stopping to kiss when one of you returns home, greet each other with a compliment, and eat meals together.
- Aim for your beloved to feel heard, understood, and accepted.
- Listen with a desire to understand.
- Find enjoyment in being close.

Secret number 34: Accept your beloved for who he or she is, not who you want him or her to be.

Snagging your Prince and Half a Kingdom. Then What?

Want to know how to hold onto the dream partner you have and make everyday communication less conflicted and more peaceful? This advice unlocks the mystery to a man's mind.

Men need to feel competent. They absolutely do not like to feel or be reminded in any way that they aren't good enough. Okay, so nor do women but here is what happens specifically for a man when you highlight any inadequacy; he could feel humiliated. Not being a fan of shame, he may then attempt to cover up his hurt and insecurity by withdrawing or becoming annoyed, firstly toward himself, and then at you, especially if you continue to discuss relationship problems with him.

Though shalt not label what you want him to do differently as being a *problem*. Refuse to call it that, and don't call it an *issue* or tell him that he needs to talk, or that you have something that needs to be *resolved*. For a man that will make his ears go all fuzzy and you will sound like a howling wolf.

1. Never tell him what he's doing is wrong. It won't make him want to change it.
2. Giving a man unwarranted advice can be seen as an attempt to put him at a disadvantage.
3. Getting him to ask or answer too many questions can make him feel weak. After all, he thinks he should have the answers.

Whatever he's not doing right won't magically dissolve just because you highlight it. Instead, how about inviting compassion in and understand that if he is doing something in a particular way, he generally has his own reasons for it. He will have a perfectly good reason. Finding out what his reasons are for doing something (or not doing something) requires understanding, patience, and time. Man timing.

For whatever reason, when some men get told they aren't performing adequately, it crushes their spirit. They feel criticized. You don't want to be triggering the thing in his emotional response centre that tells him he's not good enough. Once he is in that mind set, it may seem as though you don't stand a hope in hell of getting through, but luckily there are ways to peacefully mend this.

There are many ways to get him to work stuff out for himself. How about encouraging him to come up with his own answers as to what he thinks he may need to do better, or differently.

Developmental psychology suggests that although boy and girl brains may be wired in a particular way for language, they're also greatly influenced by parental input and the expectations of society. Many things make us what we are. Nature versus nurture is a debate that may never be fully understood. Don't give up. There are ways of encouraging change that are worth learning.

If it's a specific thing he is doing that you don't like, don't forget to search inside yourself first, and see why you are choosing to respond the way you do, and if it's actually worth bothering about. If it's something that really eats away at you, then seek to learn what his reasons are.

Perhaps, as an example, you have something you have wanted him to fix for ages and he hasn't. He may not fix it because in his mind he has ten other things that have more priority. He will have a list in his head and it will be genuine. He probably just doesn't see the need to share it with you. Women share things that are in their heads fifty times more than men. (This could be an exaggeration.) He isn't withholding to hurt you, or be difficult, he just wants to get around to it when he wants to get around to it. Why not offer to help bump something off his other list to move yours further up? How?

- Negotiate with him.
- Cajole, use humour, knock the idea around without it being a big deal and see what happens.
- Get creative. Offer to polish his sword or wash down his chariot.
- Trade sexual favours or promises of delicious feasts if you have to. They hardly ever fail.

Secret number 35: If you want to be close, be close.

Never ever say you don't feel close and need more from him. Doing that is like waving a red rag in front of a bull. It encourages defensiveness, and a defensive, criticized man will shut down. It's that simple. Don't ask for it, and don't push. Construct rather than destruct. Reach out, and be affectionate. Resurrect the things you know bring you closer. Do stuff together with fewer words.

Secret number 36: Notice what your beloved does well and compliment them on it. Praise them often, especially in front of others.

Women, how about switching things around? When he is withdrawn or reactive, know that he's not doing it *to* you. Criticizing or being forceful really doesn't work any better than trying to pull a turtle's head out of its shell. Sometimes it's better to just smile and leave him to work things out when he's ready, and choose to not be affected by it. Turtles prefer that you tickle their tummies.

Men need quiet, alone time. There are many valid man-cave activities:

- golf
- mountain biking
- gardening
- cooking
- degreasing engines
- reading
- paintball
- playing computer games
- building
- fiddling with musical instruments
- tinkering in the garage/shed

In fairytales men are always going off to save some kingdom from destruction, or hunting dragons in man-land. Man-land is important. When they are there, they are still thinking and processing, and will share what they want to share when they are ready to, and if they feel they need to. Don't be concerned; it's actually a healthy distraction, and good for both of you.

Winning your Princess and Half a Kingdom. Then What?

If your beloved happens to be a man, do him and you a great favour and either read this aloud to him, leave the page open where his curiosity will make him pick it up, or copy it and add a new catchy headline that reads something along the lines of:

Insights into the Infinite Maze of a Women's Mind.
How to Survive Emotional Outbursts of Women and Other Strange Phenomena.

Women aren't all sweet and easy to manage all of the time. Men could do with being reminded that women have an underlying need to dump off and clear out their thoughts and feelings, especially the unpleasant ones. They also need to be informed that when a woman does this, she has the power to transform from Disney Princess to something that may look and seem very *Grim* indeed. Just breathe, hope and wait, because this too shall pass.

Sometimes women empty out a lot of words simply to hear themselves, sometimes they do it to soothe themselves, and they definitely do it to get rid of any bad experience that has attached itself to them. They will want to talk and talk and talk until they are done, and only then will they leave it alone. The driving force behind their sharing is that they are seeking connection. They want to be heard and they want to feel cared for.

As a man whose initial instinct may be to automatically withdraw from conflict and ghastly experiences, this is probably scary for you. Because you might generally find it more helpful to distance yourself from uncomfortable situations in order to protect yourself, you may hope and wish she would be quiet and stop bringing the subject up. It possibly works really well for you to leave a situation behind and look to the future, but a woman will want to poke at the wasps' nest until every last one has gone and no sting is left.

It's a good idea to stop coming up with ways to make it better for her unless she asks. For a woman, that's called an interruption, and to her, it could seem like you don't really want to hear what she is saying.

If you are caught not listening, beware. It could set an alarm off in her brain that says you don't care, and if you don't care then you obviously don't love her or some such nonsense. Learn to nod and smile and come up with utterances like:

- I hear you.
- That must be terrible.
- Oh you poor thing, I hope you work it out.
- If you need me to help with anything, let me know.

You more than likely want to fix her problem so you can feel resourceful, protective, and useful. That's what knights in shining armour do. You may also want to fix it because the prince in you doesn't like seeing a damsel in distress. You just need to trust that she won't label you a failure if you don't seek to make things better. Let her talk. Let her rant and rave. Let her go until she decides she is finished. In the meantime just listen, nod, and agree with her. Parrot back some of what she is saying so she knows you are listening. Here are some words to use:

- Wow that must be awful.
- Oh, that sounds difficult.
- Gosh that's a lot to deal with.
- Are you saying...

Ask her what she wants to do about the situation, and let her talk some more. It will earn you unbelievable points. Get enough of those points and you could cash them in on a new suit of armour or some steak knives!

Ask her if she would like you to do something that might help.

Remember women use a lot more words. Sometimes they even fling their arms around. Sometimes they cry, and sometimes they get hot and bothered. Sometimes their mascara runs and they look like panda bears. Don't be concerned. That's normal. Ask her if she would like a cool drink, or some tissues, or lend her your handkerchief. Stay gallant. Don't get fearful if you witness her crumbling, it won't mean that she will become incapacitated. Vulnerability is good; it's universal in its ability to connect people. She will bounce back in time to function when she has to.

Women generally aim for intimacy and connection, and men aim for competition and independence, so in conversations that can be challenging. Actually, sharing a life together can be challenging. Luckily it's also rewarding, fun, and what most single people long to have.

Women read the minds of other women a lot. Or at least it seems like that. What they actually do is pre-empt and offer closeness with a bit more ease than men usually do. Researchers who have spent decades thoroughly studying girls and boys in regards to gender differences, say it starts at kindergarten age.

It's important to remember that children are exposed to subtle rewards and punishments that help shape their way of behaving as little princesses and princes even while they are in the womb, and that men and women begin to influence babies by their reactions and behaviours from one day old.

While you were in the sandpit comparing the size and sand-carrying capability of your toy digger, measuring it up against the little guy's one next to you, the girls were probably in the play castle making pretend cups of tea and offering to pour some for the other girls, while adjusting the curtains, and wondering if their friend might require a cushion on their seat to make them more comfortable.

Some people think it's sexist to point out obvious differences like this. Luckily those same strongly opinionated people generally don't like fairytales, so they aren't likely to be reading this book.

Probably part of the reason why we struggle with discrepancies, is that we may culturally think it's wrong to have them. We all aid gender generalizations by projecting what we think boys and girls should and shouldn't do, so we may as well get used to the results when they manifest in various ways as adults.

The idea is to embrace the differences and not expect women to be like men, and for women to not expect men to know what they want.

Secret number 37: Couples need to observe and become comfortable with each other's styles, working with, not against them.

Differences are best viewed with respect, grace, and humour. Forget about wrestling with feelings of frustration and restriction, and instead rise to the challenge. Embrace diversity; it adds interest, and variety really is the spice of life.

Secret number 38: Be open and willing to offer help because you care. Ask what might be needed of you.

Men:

If you want a five-word answer to a question rather than a paragraph or a page, then specifically request that. Say something like:

- Please tell me in five words what needs to happen with the such and such.

Women:

If you want the fairy sprinkle sandwiches cut in diagonal slices, don't just ask him to help cut them and then be disappointed or critical if he cuts them lengthwise. Be specific. Give clear instructions and ask for his commitment. Say something like:

- I need you to cut these fairy sprinkle sandwiches diagonally. Please will you do that for me?

And, men, when you get really good at it, you can ask how she would like them cut as soon as she asks for help. That will get you even more points. Three helpful tips for you:

1. Give up thinking you always know what's going on.
2. Mystery always exists.
3. There are many creative ways to a fulfilling resolution.

Secret number 39: Say I love you. Often.

- Aim to say that you love her before she says it to you.

Hopping into Bed with Frogs, Wolves and Charming Princes

This is about what could happen when you get together under the covers.

If you plan to make your relationship a lifelong one, you probably need at some point to have a discussion about children: Having children, not having children, infertility, adoption, raising the ones you have, inheriting the ones your partner brings with them, how the child you have will be stepparented, dealing with the kids you have leaving home and making their own way in the world. Whatever the topic of conversation, the undeniable key to healthy families is clear, compassionate, respectful communication.

Secret number 40: Be willing to discuss and listen to points of view that may not be the same as yours. Your magic tools are flexibility and compromise.

If you are in your relationship at the stage prior to conception, this is the time to talk about the roles that are likely to change after the birth or arrival of your child, how you will manage to share the love you have, and the consequences of doing that. Other things to discuss are finances, possible changes of circumstance, the distribution of responsibility, and what is likely to happen with work and careers. Although it may seem obvious, it's an excellent time to increase levels of understanding and safety in your relationship so that it's able to withstand big changes such as a lack of resources, and a reduction in sleep. If you iron out the creases now, it helps you know what to expect in the future. It's normal that your views will be ever-changing especially when reality hits. As long as you are willing to share ongoing ideas about religion and education, extended family involvement, sex, sports, hobbies and expectations of a hundred different kinds, all will be well.

Having a child requires patience, bravery, and dedication. Parenting is one of the hardest jobs on earth. It often demands long hours with no relief, no pay, and no overtime. The sense of responsibility and the wish for safety for your children means the job never stops, even when they grow up.

Raising a child well is a priceless contribution to society. Parenting is a journey of bravery, truth, and unconditional love.

It has been a very long time since our son *The Little Prince* Jared was a baby, but not long enough to forget the trials and tribulations that parents are confronted with. What other job sees you woken at unknown intervals to check a temperature, fetch cool flannels, empty buckets of sick, massage mysterious growing pains, or chase monsters out of the room?

Luckily the joy far outweighs the stress. Visions of our darling little creature sitting on his beanbag with his face planted in his dinner tray, almost snoring, totally exhausted from his first day at school, makes a marvellous memory imprint. No one would swap the incredible joy of seeing his first smile, hearing thousands of giggles, watching the budding of his independence, relishing his fascinating works of art, and nor would anyone have wanted to miss the buzz when new friends were made, songs were sung, and things were learnt. The flush and excitement of seeing him in love with his princess is priceless. As his parents, we like to imagine that reading fairytales together and debating things like what kind of magic seed *Thumbelina* grew from, perhaps helped grow his wonderful imagination and wicked use of words he has and uses today.

Written in 1835 by Hans Christian-Anderson, *Thumbelina* is one of the most delightful fairytales around, with a couple of priceless morals:

- People are happiest with their own kind.
- Be true to ones heart.

This tale in particular is also about empowerment and has great discussion topics that can be shared with children. It covers themes like same sex love, infertility, and creativity. In the tale, a mother longing for a child found a creative way to have one, by procuring a magical seed from a witch. When the seed grew into a baby flower girl she was greatly loved and looked after. *Thumbelina* is full of incredibly beautiful language:

"For a bed she had a walnut shell, violet petals for her mattress, and a rose petal blanket."

Everything in the tale went swimmingly well until a frog decided to steal *Thumbelina* as a bride for her son. Luckily for the wee flower girl, the birds and butterflies helped her escape. Other dangers still lay ahead, and when don't they with children? Firstly a large beetle wanted to keep her. Secondly, a spider befriended her. The beetle and the spider were fortunately persuaded by their friends to let the unusual, tiny child go. Thirdly, a field mouse tried to marry her off to a mole! A swallow bird she had previously nursed into wellness decided enough was enough, and finally rescued her properly. He took her to meet the Flower Fairy King, and she became the Flower Queen, and they, you know, lived happily ever after.

Secret number 41: Parenting is about doing the best you can, to bring a little person up to be the very best they can be.

Spiritually, parenting is a dedicated job. There is a lot that can go right, and bits that can go haywire. Oprah does a wonderful job of affirming parents by telling them she believes it's the hardest job on earth and she has interviewed thousands of people with difficult jobs.

Just to give you an idea of how hard the job can be; you have to be a multi-tasking genius, a patient teacher, an expert in nutrition, have a partial degree in the psychology of life, have medical wisdom, be part dragon-tamer and part detective, and know how to make a bed from a walnut shell. Sometimes you have to know how to replace goldfish that die, and hold funerals for pet rats.

It helps to like roller coaster rides to survive the hormonal, physical, and emotional changes you and your children go through. During many ups and downs the things that could do with staying stable are:

- consciously maintaining your loving and solid relationship; and
- making the time to nourish your dreams and care for yourself.

You can never give your children everything, but you can motivate, inspire, guide, and keep them from being carried off by toads, captured by beetles, and persuaded by mice to marry moles. Most of all you can encourage children to know how to eventually get what they need for themselves, and hope that when they grow up they will be happy.

One day My Prince
(or Princess) Shall Come

And when he or she does, if you're really lucky, or if you want it, baby makes three.

Now more than any other time in your entire relationship, is the time to step up and be the most important person in each other's lives. Even when and if sex and sleep are off the agenda, remember to reach deep within to your reserve resources and make an extra effort to connect with each other.

Having a baby means signing up for the complete package, and part of that package means learning to cope with being woken repeatedly in the night, obtaining an extra work load, and sharing love that once just belonged between the two of you.

You may want to get people on board to help with practicalities, although be aware that for some, it can be a strain sharing your house with extended family members, especially ones with strong opinions or judgements. Why not hire help if you are able to? There has to be a fairy godmother floating around somewhere? A fairy godmother archetype is one who provides extravagant and benevolent gifts, but does not remain involved or enmeshed in your life. Sounds perfect. She or he can come in many shapes and sizes. The only dead give a way is the magic wand, and maybe the wings and the trail of glitter.

This brand spanking new time in your lives is a wonderful opportunity to bring fresh energy, vitality, and new connections into your home or castle. It's the beginning of a new stage, a deepening of what you had before, rather than the end of freedom. Being a parent can bring out welcoming, previously undiscovered character traits. It has been known to turn the odd cold frog into a warm-hearted mushy marshmallow and a few grouchy bears into pussycats.

For a while it helps if you change the order of things that might normally take precedence. Move your relationship into first place, your family into second, personal third, work into fourth, and your friendships and outside interests into fifth.

If the focus isn't on the relationship, there is a danger of intimacy slipping. It is vitally important to sleep together in the same bed, to cuddle, to be close, and to share the joys and challenges of your brand new experience. You are in this together. Some people describe becoming a parent for the first time as a culture shock and say they had no idea how life changing it would be. They also say they wouldn't trade it.

For self-preservation it's important to remember what you did in your life before, what interests you had, and what dreams and future plans you looked forward to, and hold out hope that you can do them again, or come up with a suitable revision.

Make an effort to avoid becoming less important to each other. Forget interacting in an ordinary way, the way you might with anyone else in average day-to-day living. You have created a family. You made magic. What you have is special. It's what some people long for, so why not give what you have a hundred percent investment. Value each other, say lovely things, be sexy, be silly, be naughty, and definitely be intimate. Love in a deeply abiding way. Share with each other on a level that you wouldn't dream of with anyone else. Spill love directly from your heart. You owe it to the future happiness of your little prince or princess to reconnect. Try not to focus all your conversations on the baby and what they are doing or not doing. Remember all the other things that bond you and your beloved together.

As the queen, make sure you let him or her know what you need them to do. Talk about plans that could offer you relief, and find some kind of sharing system that works when it comes to childcare duties. Hopefully the king or queen won't be jealous of the time you get to spend bonding, feeding, and caring for the little prince or princess. Best he or she joins in by bonding too. It's likely that a combination of lack of sleep and the absolute attention the baby needs, can make you feel jet-lagged and emotional, so welcome all the support that comes your way.

As parents, try not to tiptoe around. Let babies get used to noise. Let other people get used to the fact that babies make noise. They can fit in with your life and survive and thrive. Know that having children can affect some of your friendships.

Lack of sleep for parents can sometimes feel like a descent into hell. Lots of couples say it can last for at least six months. The gratefulness felt when a baby sleeps through the night can feel like another miracle. When and if things feel difficult, keep bonding as a couple.

Remember that it's all part of a great timeline, a measure, so that when things get easier (and they will) you can laugh together about how difficult things were in the early days and marvel at how amazing you were to overcome it. Practically speaking, one of you could lessen the stress and buy some great earplugs and take turns catching up on dreamtime.

Although most people are willing to share gruesome stories of giving birth, not many feel safe enough to share how tough the adjustment to being a parent is, or how vulnerable they may feel in the first six weeks to six months. Of course it varies for different people, but it's not uncommon for people to not want to appear unable to cope.

There is unfortunately no paint-by-numbers parenting rulebook. Some people find it easy. Some don't. All babies have different temperaments and sleep patterns. They cry for many different reasons, and mostly you get to work through a process of elimination until you discover the exact reason. Little critters are so vulnerable and require so much in the early days. Keep trusting that together you can come up with creative plans on how to offer relief, make things easier, more productive, and fun.

If extended family is staying, enjoy their contributions. Let them cook. Get them to take the baby for a walk while you have a bath together (if stitches allow) or just sit down and soak up kind offers of footbaths and head and shoulder massages.

Talk and bring up fun things to do in the future. Maybe as a couple, you could get bits of paper and crayons and write:

- what your hopes and dreams are;
- where you see yourself in five years time;
- what improvements can be made on your castle; and
- which kingdom you might wish to visit next.

Having super things to look forward to, while treasuring the moment, makes a significant difference in keeping your spirits up.

Continue to stay connected and interested in each other's day. It's far too easy to be separate if you feel you are missing out on something from your old life.

Make time after the initial adjustment period to still have a **date night**. If the baby is tiny, try leaving it during the day at sleep time (maybe not in a walnut shell) with someone you trust and go out for lunch or breakfast as a couple.

Even with so many changes and such pressure, one of the most helpful things to remember is:

Secret number 42: It's vital that you treat each other with the utmost respect, and continue to treat each other as though you are the most precious valuable treasure ever.

The bottom line is you have to love. You have to love fully, no matter what, because anything else is a rip off. There has to be exquisite pleasure. Grab the delight that life brings.

Avoid being separate in order to avoid pain and loss down the track. Forget about becoming distant. Move in closer than ever, and enjoy this moment in time. Now is the absolute best time you could do with gifting each other every day, with a glimmer of gratitude.

- Make a list of at least five emotionally and physically fulfilling things that would make you happy to receive from each other.

If it feels like a really challenging phase, know that this is such a short period in your long timeline of life. All fairytales have challenges, followed by turning points, and finally some kind of resolution that gives you a new understanding of yourself.

You are so capable of creative solutions and you will get through this time with many fabulous memories, funny photographs, wicked stories, and dribble stains.

This experience will help you resolve other difficult times you may face in the future. Believe you can work through it, and you will.

Whether it's your second child or your seventh, remember to talk about how it could change your day-to-day living. Come up with constructive and caring solutions, and keep in mind that cementing your bond makes everything easier.

You may have the added consideration of getting other children used to another baby. Things that are proven to help siblings adjust to new arrivals are:

- encouraging caring behaviours;
- sharing attention;
- making sure you tell each child how and why they are special to you;
- brainstorming names and involving them in the fun process;
- asking them which fairytale character names are their favourites and why;
- getting them to explain why they named their toys the way they did;
- encouraging him or her to talk about what they are most looking forward to and what they are dreading or fearing;
- teaching them about the different stages of pregnancy;
- talking about the baby when it's in the hatching mode;
- showing him or her age-appropriate pictures of the hatching stages;
- letting them feel the baby kick;
- showing them scans;
- planning special things to do when their little sibling comes home;
- getting them to make artwork or craft for the babies room;
- allowing them to take on certain responsibilities; and
- giving him or her meaningful helping jobs.

Watch with joy as he or she finds ways to bond with the baby in his or her own magnificent way.

"If you want your children to be intelligent, read them fairy tales. If you want them to be more intelligent, read them more fairy tales."
Albert Einstein.

Ogres, stepparents, and evil plots

Love your life, live your best life, have confidence, keep a cool head, and your survival within a blended family is pretty much assured. Easier said than done, but if you calmly choose to work through difficulties and remember to celebrate all of the good times, you'll do a great job and hopefully be rewarded with a happy ending for all.

All parents, in fact all grown-ups have the ability to act in ways that can frighten children. We as adults could do with being aware every day, in every moment, of how our actions and words impact children. Luckily through listening to, and reading fairytales, clued-up children usually learn how to get their own back. They know that it's not okay for ogres to harass or bully others, and that curses can be fixed by quests or by getting some expert assistance from magical or wise helpers who are pretty good at ensuring that their wishes come true.

Historically in real life, many women pregnant in the 1800's when certain fairytales were penned, died in childbirth, so there were a lot of fathers with children who remarried. Times were harsh. With many mouths to feed and extremely gruelling time-consuming household chores to attend to, survival was at the forefront. The guys needed help, so maybe a big percentage of them remarried thinking more about getting practical needs met, than ensuring that the emotional needs of their children were provided for? That's probably why wicked stepmothers in particular, featured rather strongly in fairytales. Look at the meanies in *Cinderella*, *Snow White* and *Hansel and Gretel*.

In a lot of those tales, a lot of the time, the arguments were around food. Back then it was more about avoiding hunger, filling ones belly, and desiring to eat a child or two! Our stresses now pale in comparison, reduced to the odd fight at the dinner table trying to get a distressed teenage princess to maybe eat enough, or keep her food down, or begging a child to stop communicating on social media long enough to join the family for a shared meal.

Secret number 43: Children learn from what they see, not from what you say.

Children love to imitate. It's a bit of a case of monkey see, monkey do! Parents and stepparents are role models, so when we love what we do and we love and accept who we are, children stand a really great chance of doing the same. It's paramount that adult relationships are strong and united. The stronger you both are, the more secure children will feel. Try not to let a child interfere in your relationship. Remember that a good re-marriage or re-partnering is about *your* love. Children never have a say in that, so it may take them longer to fit in. They require time to grieve and to adjust to changes like their original parent not being present all the time. They may still only want to share private feelings with one parent and if that's not you, it can be hard for both of you. While it's great to expose them to your strong, healthy, loving, new relationship, they may still worry about things like abandonment, or fear betraying the original parent as they grow to like the replacement. Try to avoid power struggles wherever possible.

It's our job as a parent to know what's best for our children. It's our task to keep them safe from others and safe from themselves. Grown-ups have to decide lots of things for children. A parent's role is to love, nurture, create boundaries, teach, and live by example. (And to make sure there's no sitting in cinders, unjust oppression or any taunting going on.) Sometimes it feels mean to make difficult decisions or to stop them from doing some of the things they want to do. Just remember you really do know best.

You are the best judge of his or her safety. You know that if they stay out after midnight:

- the carriage will turn back into a pumpkin and they could get embarrassed;
- the streets at night are full of dangerous rogues, foolish tricksters, and wild wolves with huge sexual appetites that aren't to be trusted; and
- it will cost you or them a fortune in taxi fares once they realize a pumpkin without wheels won't get them home!

You know about the sorts of things that aren't going to serve them in the long run, so go ahead and enforce the rules fairly. Put forward good reasons.

As hard as it is to do, it's not your job to be his or her friend. If friendship comes later, then that's great, it'll be a bonus.

It's a stepparent's job to back you in your decisions.

Obviously there will be many things that you will both need to discuss privately out of the children's earshot.

Whatever you do, refuse to operate out of guilt. Don't be too lenient or overindulge them just because you might feel bad or guilty that they are missing out on growing up with, and spending the kind of time that they used to, with their original mum and dad. Children are resilient. In an environment of love, kindness and respect, they know how to find their way, are capable of learning new survival skills, and will adjust given time.

Important points to remember:

- Never argue in front of your children. Arguing changes who they are.
- When you discuss how to parent them, don't do it in front of them.
- Don't show them any weak links.
- Decide on what's acceptable and what's not acceptable.
- Make the rules clear.
- Make the rules fair.
- Always follow through with consequences. Consequences need to be immediate and reasonable for their age.
- Rules need to be set and delivered to children by the parent, not the stepparent.
- In no way should a stepparent step forward and initiate discipline.
- Stepparent means one step back.

As a stepparent:

- Your role is to learn how to be a team, to have consistency and follow through.
- Allow the parent to parent.
- Don't be jealous of the relationship a child has with their real parent.
- Never force children to call stepsibling's brothers and sisters.
- Never force them to call you mum or dad. Have them find a name that fits.
- Show sincere interest.
- Be patient with the child.
- Give yourself time to get to know them.
- Learn what he or she loves and needs.
- Be yourself.

- Be authentic rather than be tempted to play a role in order to be liked or accepted.
- Allow children to express love for the absent parent.
- Never feel like love is a competition.

It could be likely that your child or children will buck the system a little more, especially in the beginning stages of blending a family, so it's even more vital that you stay calm when disciplining.

- Use your voice not force, and watch out for the ogre within!
- Tell him or her why they can't do whatever they are doing.
- They need to know what you expect from them, and what the likely consequences will be if they push limits and boundaries.

Be direct, consistent and confident:

- Tell them it's not okay to hit you, or talk to you in ways that are unacceptable.
- Deliver your message and walk away.
- Ignore any pleas for attention when he or she is in time-out.
- Time-out needs to be timed and undertaken somewhere non-stimulating. Don't send them to their room. Use a naughty chair or step. Set a timer for one minute for every year of age he or she is. Two minutes for two year olds, ten minutes for ten year olds. Sit them down and ask them to think about their behaviour.
- When their time is up, ask them to tell you why they got sent to time-out, and see if they are ready to apologize.
- Then let it go and be nice. Keep things upbeat, positive, and loving.
- Remember it's only his or her behaviour you don't approve of. Let them know that you still love them.

Wicked Witches and
Axe-wielding Woodsmen

If you are finding it a struggle adjusting to being separated or divorced and you have children, you owe it to them to make up and move on. It's an annoying reality, but anything you found difficult when you were with your ex is likely to be amplified now you are apart. If you weren't able to resolve certain things when you were together, your chances of being able to now is next to nil unless you are prepared to compromise, breathe, and change. You may be lucky enough to own a magic wand. If so, good for you, transformation may come more easily. Better that than an axe!

Once you separate or divorce, you immediately lose the same rights you once had. It's the children who have rights now. You get to concede that whatever difficulty you had may never be resolved, but it can be dissolved if and when you choose to let it go.

Reacting emotionally has a bad habit of pouring fuel on a fire. The desire for revenge can often be so great that it can turn seemingly level headed people into grudge holding monsters. Just keep working on feeling secure in your self and your decisions. Insecurity has a way of creating anxious, angry, and controlling behaviours. Trust that time will heal things. Have faith in your ability to be calm.

Whenever there are children involved, calm and respectful communication needs to be established. Children can suffer if they are dragged into post-relationship arguments. It is traumatic for children to hear constant put-downs about someone to whom they are intrinsically linked. They don't need to know that you think your ex is a wicked witch or an axe-wielding woodsman.

Secret number 44: If you condemn and dismiss your ex and your child hears it, you are in essence rejecting your child.

We can move on. Children can't. They still have the genes of our former partner. Our issues are our issues and it doesn't matter how much someone may have wronged us, it's not good for children to hear or know what those issues are. Children are a piece of each of their parents.

No matter what situation you find yourself in now, you and your ex once created your child together, out of love. That should never be taken away from a child, even if you dislike your ex immensely.

Spitting tacks at each other is distressing, and can have long-term negative effects on an innocent child. Children need stability, safety, and routine. They need emotional safety to be able to share their concerns. They may not share anything with you if they think you will use what they say as ammunition, or if it might jeopardize their relationship with their other parent, who they will hopefully continue to love no matter what has transpired between the two of you. Never ask them to keep a secret.

Secret number 45: Children are not bargaining chips. Access should never be restricted simply to force demands, or to punish the other party. Your child's welfare is paramount.

Unless there are severe circumstances like danger to life and safety, it has been acknowledged by many experts that both parents should continue to play a joint role in the life of the child. You may not like it, but major decisions regarding religion, culture, education, and medical treatment are the sorts of things you need to jointly decide on for a long time, forever after even.

What really helps, is to move to a position of acceptance. The role you and your ex now play with each other is only that of shared parents of the child or children you created.

If you find you can't yet manage to hold your tongue or reserve your judgements, then only communicate with your ex when you have to. Keep to the topic at hand. Stick to facts rather than feelings, and aim for resolution and harmony. Breathe a lot. Right down deep into your belly.

You could organize and arrange for smooth handovers where you have minimal involvement with each other. Choose a place like childcare or school, or that of an extended family member, or mutual friend. Or the pick-up parent could simply sound the car horn at the gate at home. Smile and wave and stay quiet, or tell them to have a really great time, so the child sees you are comfortable with what they are doing, and that you support where they are going and who they are going with.

You could pre-arrange telephone calls when the child knows they can answer the phone, or the child could communicate online with the other parent.

Strive to handle all these times calmly and fairly.

Be a generous spirit where you can. Let dad have the child on Father's Day and mum have them on Mother's Day. Where it is practical, share other special days.

Consider keeping a beautiful book that can travel to both houses with the child. It can be filled with happy things worth sharing, and used to highlight positive experiences, milestones, and awards. Your child could decorate it and name it something really cool. Things worth sticking in the book are positive stories of time spent with each parent, fabulous drawings of fun things, and a list of friends addresses and phone numbers for unexpected things like parties that pop up. Make sure there is a page in there that reads: Things that are good for me.

This is where they write the time they know they are meant to go to bed, the time they need to get up, how much time is acceptable on the computer or in front of the television. It's also a fun and thoughtful place to list things like:

- I brush my teeth after breakfast, and before I go to sleep.
- I am supposed to drink water, not sugary soda.
- I remember to say please and thank you to people.
- I use polite language and respect my elders.
- I tell the truth.
- I always buckle my seatbelt.

Have fun coming up with other important values and boundaries.

If you are keeping communication minimal, this book is vital to respectfully instruct the other parent about current medicine dosages, specific requirements, and urgent things that need attending to. Make sure doctors and dentists, school phone numbers, favourite fairytales, and extended family members contact names and numbers are in there and clearly listed.

Fifty Ingredients in

Share what you think, and believe ♥ Be intimate

Be compassionate ♥ Respect yourself

Believe in yourself, your talents and strengths

Respect others ♥ Have and respect clear boundaries

COMMUNICATE CLEARLY ♥ Be curious, open, and interested

Wait for your turn to talk ♥ Have fun

Desire connection ♥ Trust in life's ups and downs

Support the dreams of others ♥ Encourage

Praise ♥ Create things to look forward to

Know when to be gentle or assertive

Be genuine ♥ Express yourself candidly

Nurture yourself ♥ LIVE FULLY ♥ Nurture others

Be creative ♥ Act with faith, hope, and charity

the Elixir of Love

Self first, love second, family third 🖤 Bend & flex

EMBRACE REALITY 🖤 Balance self-sufficiency & independence

Admire differences 🖤 Make each day a new day

Live now. Thank the past. Get excited about the future

Be loving & loveable 🖤 Believe in goodness

Think clearly, feel deeply, act wisely 🖤 BE PATIENT

Act responsibly 🖤 Happiness is a choice

Be loyal 🖤 Connect intimately every single day

Forgive and make amends 🖤 Be sensual & sexual

Surrender graciously 🖤 Share your hopes & dreams

Feed your soul 🖤 Every action has a consequence

Embrace reality 🖤 Fill your world with joy

Speak to others with love. 🖤 Believe in happily ever after

Part THREE

Fixing Crumbling Castles

Turning Castles into Palaces

Most relationships at some stage need fixing. Part three covers mending what's busted so that what you have and value, doesn't go to rack and ruin. Nothing ever has to be totally demolished. Even crumbling castles.

Welcome to extreme makeover castle edition! Sometimes when we don't feel we're getting what we want, the foundations that we cleverly strengthened in *Aiming for 'Just Right'* can get a little shaky. If they wobble about for too long, cracks can start showing in all kinds of places, so it's now time to learn about reinforcing.

If things are going wrong and you want a strong magnificent mansion, consider learning how to:

- mix plaster;
- study a new set of palace plans;
- rally up a bit of extra support; and
- maybe bring in the repair experts.

With the exception of a few deal breakers, most serious situations can be resolved. Finding new, appropriate, and fitting responses when you are out of your depth or faced with obstacles, can be challenging. Luckily it's not impossible.

Significant changes are possible when you are willing to do the work and focus on a positive result.

At the end of part three, *Fixing Crumbling Castles*, you will be ready to yell: "Drivers (all six of you mice) move that pumpkin!"

Study the DIY on dysfunctional behaviours which follows to help identify where your difficulties may have come from, what to do if you have them, or what to do if you live with someone that has them.

DIY - Dysfunctional Behaviour

Difficult behaviours:	In order for you to change your behaviour this is what you could do:	If you live with someone with these behaviours, this is what you could do:
Anxiety	Confront your fear and understand it.Release tension. Be in the present moment and accept that change is constant. Seek happiness. Cultivate confidence. Focus on what you can do well.	Reassure them. Help them focus on the present moment, and affirm their ability to deal with whatever life deals them. Don't pressure them.
Feeling guilty a lot	Don't overcompensate. Who you are and what you do is enough. Just be okay with giving the gift of yourself. Guilt is when you overstep your own boundaries.	Tell them they say sorry too much. Ask them what they think they might need to do in order to not have to apologize after they have done something.
Walled off or depressed	Let your anger out. Don't be angry with yourself. Trust that you can protect yourself and stand up for yourself. Initiate something today, and see that you are wonderful. Relax. Seek closeness and curiosity. Discover the energy that comes with action.	Let them know that it's okay to need you. Tell them that love includes reaching out and being supported even if it feels difficult. Don't give up on them. Stay connected. Encourage them to move their body and use their mind.

Disappointed	Learn to ask for help. Look to see what payoff there is for feeling like a victim. Step up to an empowered way of being and get your needs met without manipulating. Look at whether you are surrounded by the right kind of people. Aim to be victorious rather than victimized. Look at things from a positive angle.	Get them to find solutions for themself, to creatively brainstorm what they need, when they need it, and why they need it.
Victim of abuse	Acknowledge your past and delight in who you are now. Celebrate your successes. Pay attention to one feeling at a time. Participate fully in life. Rebuild trust. Say no without guilt or fear. Create stability and security. Make time to play. Invite innocence into your life. Set boundaries. Think for yourself, and be your own wise counsel.	Be respectful of their boundaries. Ask them what their triggers are. Work out what things you could avoid doing, and think about places you could avoid going, so they know you care. Confront them if they act abusively to you, or others, or they are self-abusing.
Self destructive	Recognize destructive behaviours. Replace with positive behaviours. Treat yourself with respect. Recognize that your behaviour affects others. You are responsible for being kind to yourself. Seek help. Feel.	Challenge unhealthy actions. Book them in with an expert if they are self-harming. Remove dangerous things. Boost their self-esteem with lots of praise. Tell them you know they are capable of kindness.

Drawn to chaos and catastrophe	Ask questions. Gather adult information, slowly, and mindfully. Focus on what's good in your life. Put your surroundings in order. Clear through rubble, both physical and emotional. Seek solitude and calm. Allow yourself to feel. Surround yourself with tranquil images. Spend some time in serene, peaceful environments.	Don't buy into it. Don't fight or argue. Ask who, what, when, why, and how questions to get them to think their way through drama. Praise them when they are calm and clear thinking. Set boundaries. Encourage them to be, rather than do.
Expecting rejection	Recognize how much you bring to a relationship. Who you are is good enough. Affirm to yourself how good you are, how worthy you are to be with. Trust that you are worth being with. You have no control over other people's actions, only your own. Be there for yourself. Be self-caring and follow your dreams. Visualize yourself happy. See yourself fitting in.	A difference of opinion doesn't mean you are withdrawing your love, so make them at ease. Offer reassurance when they least expect it. People who expect to be abandoned often abandon themselves. Ask them to stop behaviours that push you away. Tell them how much they mean to you and how much you love having them around. Let them know they add value to your life. Encourage happy, connected times.

Fighting Combative Defiant	Stop violating boundaries. Look at what you get from provoking others and fighting back, and get that in a new way. Seek peace. Ask gentle, enquiring questions to get the answers you want. Ask yourself: If I say this in this way, what is the likely response? If I have peace, what would I then have to focus on in my life? Look at your attitude to authority. Ask others for their ideas. Listen. Be respectful.	Ask what they are afraid of. Refuse to enter into an argument. Don't justify and defend. Ask gentle enquiring questions, and listen fully. If what they are saying isn't clear, ask them to say it again in a calm respectful way that will make you want to listen. They are unconsciously pushing you away so don't buy into it by running. Stay put, and get them to look at their own behaviour.
Smothering	Be there for yourself. Think for yourself. Find things to do for yourself that consumes you in a positive way. Be your own wise counsel. Explore. Seek freedom, and allow freedom. Let go of control. Rebuild your trust. Holding on too tight means you don't trust that you are loving and loveable enough.	Make a schedule that includes quality relationship time, and quality self time. Inform where you are and what you are doing until they get used to it. Those who have nothing to hide, hide nothing. Encourage them to find activities they love to do, and praise them when they act independently.

Being right Judgemental	Face up to your feelings of inadequacy. Build your self worth. Others have a right to be who they are and do what they do. Seek to find what makes you happy. Allow others their input. Just listen and breathe, and know that you don't have to respond. Remember that opinion is not truth.	Agree to disagree. Avoid conflict. Don't take the bait. Respond by saying "You have very strong views" or "Gosh it's interesting that you feel that way." Ask them if they want to be right or happy. See that underneath their bravado they are unsure of themselves.
Acting crazy	Balance your head and your heart. Find appropriate actions for uncomfortable feelings. Find serenity and harmony. Ask clear questions and set plain limits. Don't overdo stimulants. Do breathing exercises, and take up yoga. Be brave and trust your ability to deal with life.	Don't fear it. Have rescue remedy on hand. Calmly encourage them. Say you trust that they can handle all situations in a sane and calm way. See that acting crazy is a cop out. Tell them that life won't give them anything they can't actually handle.
Lying	Get used to anger and disapproval. Learn to trust that you can cope with anything that comes your way. Take responsibility for your actions, and think before you act so you reduce the consequences to your actions. Accept the truth.	Ask what they are afraid of if you find out the truth. What response are they expecting? See if you can increase safety for them by asking what they think is an appropriate consequence for their actions. Let them know that one lie discovered has the ability to make you question the validity of everything.

Bitterness	Release resentment. Explore forgiveness even if it's through meditation. Laugh. Focus on today and what you have to look forward to. Soften your heart. Smile more often. Dream.	Increase joy. Watch cartoons. Laugh a lot. Encourage smiles. Encourage them to find ways to release old anger. Try a game of darts, find a patch of weeds to destroy, throw stones, kick a ball, walk fast, or demolish something.
Dependant Needy Demanding	Know what you need. Let go. Trust that your own decisions can guide you. Be content with alone time. Aim for balance in giving and receiving. Give yourself positive messages. Acknowledge your gifts, and honour your intelligence. Learn the skills you need to be independent. Take space and allow others space.	Praise their independent actions, and tell them you find it empowering and attractive when they care for themselves. Make yourself unavailable for their every drama. Encourage them to seek guidance from someone other than you. Ask them how they expect to fix it.
Overly responsible	Affirm your own uniqueness. Learn to lean on others for support. Ask for help. Be tender and loving towards yourself. Try new things. Be willing to experiment. Be silly. Let go. Trust others. Someone else can take over the reins. Get a shoulder massage. Float in the ocean. Ride a roller coaster. Blow bubbles. Take up yoga. Hand over problems to the universe.	Ask, "How can I help you" and mean it. Make them stop and slow down. Touch does this quite quickly. Add spontaneity to the day. Don't ask; just take over a task for them. Invite play into situations. Listen to their concerns, and try to encourage them to let go. Tell them you are capable of not only caring for yourself, but more than able to take the reins for both of you sometimes.

Perfectionist	Allow others to be themselves. Look for joy. Learn to do nothing. Slow down. Be silly. Mistakes are acceptable. Growth occurs through errors. What is the worst that could happen if you screw up? Forgive yourself. Forgive others. Know that feelings don't get a chance to surface when you are fussing. Stop hiding. Be real. Change how high you set the bar.	Encourage games where you both get things wrong and can laugh about it, or games where you get dirty and survive. Book a roller coaster ride, a haunted house experience. Pack a picnic with no knives and forks. Love them for who they are.
Blaming others	Feel your true feelings and express them respectfully and appropriately. Search to see if your behaviour needs to change. Let go of expectations. Look at your own hurt and fears. Solve whatever the problem is and move on. Take responsibility. Look for the silver lining.	Ask them to stop and name what they feel rather than focus on what you did or didn't do. Ask what they need from you. Ask them to be respectful. Get them to stay calm and to own what they say. Ask them what needs to happen to heal the grievance.
Manipulating others Whining Complaining	Find out what is wrong and fix it yourself. Be honest. Know what you need and learn to ask others to meet your needs directly. Don't use a third party. Be civil. Ask slowly and clearly with a neutral tone. Share what you feel. Don't be afraid of your own anger.	No means no. Don't give in if your boundaries are realistic. Don't pacify them with stuff. Ask them to ask you in a way that gets a positive result. Ask them to use a tone that works. Respond positively to their pleasant behaviour.

Living in fantasy	Face the truth. Feel your feelings. Grieve. Find order if you have chaos. Stay in the present moment, in the present day, and be content with reality. Look at who needs you, who you are not present for, and how that might affect them when you engage in behaviours that make you unavailable. Check to see if your fantasy is actually an addiction that needs attending to.	Set realistic time limits and blow their cover. Let them know you know what they are doing and say you prefer it when they are honest and present. Tell them when they hurt you. Ask them to connect and mean it.
Being a martyr	Find your own sense of purpose. Say no to others and say yes to yourself. Uncover new interests. Pamper yourself. Save yourself. Seek support. Be creative. Take the pressure off. Rest, eat at proper times, and reassure yourself that you are enough. Discard rules. Let anger out. Play. Be inspired. Play some more.	When they are not exhausted, praise them for their ability to care for themself. Tell them you love it when they do nice things for themselves. Tell them you are more than happy and capable of taking care of yourself. Encourage fun things. Don't buy into any stress or chaos.

Being a victim	Replace despair with hope. Speak out with conviction and courage. Face fears and act in spite of them. Enforce boundaries. Make your environment safe. Gather information and support on how to deal with what is happening, or what has happened. Don't be bullied. Seek help from an expert so you can fight back, protect yourself, or stay away. Don't isolate yourself. Never blame yourself. When people do bad things, know that it stems from their own feelings of insecurity and worthlessness. Keep a note of any incidents that concern you. Read as many articles as you can on how others have coped in similar situations to you.	Listen and support them. Validate their experience. Encourage courage, and help them fight their battle. Being bullied or victimized is horrible so don't get bored with their stories, they are real. Never be an idle bystander. Tell them it's okay to tell authorities that can enforce change. If they need to walk away from a situation, support their decision.
Addiction	Find a spiritual purpose. Fill your emptiness another way. Replace a bad habit with a good one. Aim for serenity. Seek healthy adventure. Affect change within yourself. Wake up to the reality of the present moment. Trust. Go to rehab and work the programme wisely.	This one is up to them, not you. Don't support or encourage their addiction financially, or emotionally. Support their recovery and treatment, and say you know they are capable of good choices.

Sweetest Tongue has Sharpest Tooth

"Little girls, this seems to say, never stop upon your way, never trust a stranger-friend; no one knows how it will end. As you're pretty so be wise; wolves may lurk in every guise. Handsome they may be, and kind, gay, and charming, never mind! Now, as then, tis simple truth, sweetest tongue has sharpest tooth!"
Charles Perrault.

In *Little Red Riding Hood,* apart from the most common message about remaining chaste and watching out for sweet-talking wolves who might want to follow us home and ravage us, the other message we are reminded about, is to never stop upon our way. The tale tells how easily it is to get distracted from our own goals, and encourages us to call on inner wisdom to make our own journey a priority, and to be certain of who helps us and who hinders us along our way.

Sacrificing ones own needs is a sure fire way to become derailed. Knowing how to manage difficulties that pop up and frighten us is vital for our emotional survival. Staying empowered and checking in on our own needs can help eliminate passive responses that leave us feeling as though we have to do what someone else wants. Doing what other people want us to do when we don't really want to, too often creates aggressive behaviours. Assertiveness and good self-awareness, mixed in with a touch of street skill, enables healthier coping strategies, helps maintain composure, and gets the basket of goodies to Grandma's house without distraction. No matter how clever we think we are, conflict can show up on whatever path we take. It's just one of those unavoidable things in life and love, and yet it is often through experiencing painful processes that we end up learning the most about others and ourselves.

The wolf wanted to eat *Little Red Riding Hood,* but was clearly not willing to do so in public. This is why it's a very good idea to bring up difficult conversations in public places. It's safer. In public, your beloved and you get to socially conform and communicate in a sweeter way even if there are sharp teeth gnashing behind the smile. Saliva can drip all it wants, but in public, niceness prevails. Conversing over a coffee in a café with other customers within listening distance helps calm the snarl and allows sweetness to surface. It also ensures that if someone wants to take a bite there's generally a good chance of intervention in the form of a protective lumberjack type, who is bound to want to jump in and cut things down the middle.

Meeting up to spend time together needn't always involve sharing deep and meaningful feelings. Sometimes it's better to be less intense. Talking about how you feel about each other, to each other, and always having to resolve things can be both threatening and boring. What about sharing how you feel about things going on in the community, and in the world at large?

The crucial thing is to be present and look at each other when you are talking or listening and:

- express concern;
- stay curious;
- be creative;
- explore;
- investigate;
- observe;
- predict;
- raise questions, and
- use icebreakers.

Inject fun into your conversations by asking, "Imagine if?" "What would you do if?"

When we want to know more, we encourage a natural urge in others to communicate their discoveries. When others aren't busy justifying or defending, they don't have to bare their sharp teeth as a protection mechanism. Respecting and valuing their answers actually creates safety.

Secret number 46: When communicating, leave space for answers so that new ideas can sprout, blossom, and branch off in all kinds of new directions.

We must keep the need to scramble to have our say in a hurried way, in check. Otherwise it can come across as though we aren't really listening or weighing carefully what someone else has to say. Being competitive, wanting to get one up on others, or seeking to have the best story to tell, is bad manners. Not quite as bad manners as the wolf conning *Little Red Riding Hood* into picking flowers so he could rush ahead and disguise himself as Grandma, with the underlying intention of gobbling Red up as soon as she leaned in a little too close. When communicating, practise waiting your turn. Life is long. Trust that there will be many chances to say what you want to say, and plenty of time and opportunity to do it when you are patient with yourself and others.

Sometimes it's only one person from the relationship who comes to therapy. Often times they will say they feel they are being disloyal, straying off the path to seek outside help. They also have a tendency to overly explain that their beloved isn't a big bad wolf. Luckily in therapy, the needs of partners who aren't present are respected, honoured, and considered. It doesn't always take both people to change a dynamic. Even if it's only you that wants to work at making things better, it's possible to do so. People often ask why it is that they have to do all the work. The answer is simple: Because you're the one that wants to. You wouldn't be looking for help if you didn't think it was possible. There's always a way. The determined shall eventually be rewarded. Your awareness, your eagerness for improvement, your commitment to take responsibility and make change happen, can set off a positive ripple effect.

Secret number 47: Unearth the uncomfortable feelings that get activated in you, rather than focusing on what someone does to irritate or annoy you.

If we continue to concentrate on things that other people do to annoy, irritate, or aggravate us, and if we highlight and chew over it long enough, it magnifies a problem and can lead to more conflict and disappointment. Pointing the finger, blaming, and feeling ripped off, is never the recipe for success.

It's not possible to give or receive love if we are in a blaming or criticizing cycle. Most of the time couples try, wish, and hope to change each other, instead of taking a look within to see what they might need to change about themselves. If and when you feel like you're not getting what you want, look at what begins to surface in relation to how you believe you are being treated. Then, work out if your feelings are rational, whether they are old and familiar, or whether they are warranted. See if there's anything about your behaviour that needs to change, or could change, to create more constructive situations. If *Little Red Riding Hood* wasn't such a naïve, people (or wolf) pleaser, she would have shared a lot less information. In turn that could have kept her out of danger and she wouldn't have needed rescuing. Sure the wolf may have found another target, that's always a little harder to stop.

Secret number 48: Always aim to construct, rather than destruct.

To diffuse conflict, it's helpful to believe in and value harmony.

- Think about what you are saying and what your intention is.
- What drives you to say it?
- What result do you desire?
- How can you best achieve that?

The golden rules:

- Be willing to apologize.
- Never be dishonest.
- Check your own mood.
- See if you are being reasonable.
- Put your sharp wolf teeth away.
- Explain what's wrong in a calm manner.
- Watch your tone.
- An underlying snarl is not sweet talk.
- Don't trick or con.
- Clarify and understand their perspective.
- Find the courage to be vulnerable.
- Resist the temptation to threaten, intimidate or terrorize.
- Be tolerant.
- Stay hopeful.
- Reduce altercations.
- Inject some magic or nonsense into the mix.
- Change the channel.
- As always, aim to treat each other with respect.

Secret number 49: Never give your power over to anyone else. (Especially to a conman or a big bad wolf).

How to become more self-empowered when relating to others:

- Examine your feelings.
- Trust your intuition.
- Share what you discover, without fearing consequences.
- Don't converse if you have a hunch not too.
- Believe that what other people think of you is none of your business.
- Understand that a difference of opinion is not a withdrawal of love.
- You can always agree to disagree, and still keep a smile on your face.
- Stay authentic.
- Practice openness.
- Listen with your heart.
- Listen with your ears, and instinct.
- Make it easy for your beloved to tell you things that are uncomfortable.
- When they do, be accepting and gracious.
- Thank and praise others for their honesty.
- Know that you and the relationship can survive lumps, bumps, crooked paths, rocky roads, wild animal encounters, and challenges.
- Keep being a safe person to be around.
- Stay in the moment as much as possible.
- Be less hyper-vigilant.
- Trust that you can both share difficult feelings and find a way through to an enlightened clearing.
- Stay clear-headed.
- Sort out the wood from the trees.
- Knowing what's what and where you all stand makes it easier to resolve differences.

Beauty and the Beast

Belle was pure of heart. She had two sisters who were wicked and selfish. When their father went on his trip of a lifetime, he asked what gift he could bring home for them. Belle asked for a rare rose and surprise, surprise, her sisters asked for jewels and fine dresses. Their father sadly fell upon hard times when he was away, and little by little, lost all of his wealth. One day he found himself wandering around in a storm, and ended up outside a wonderful mansion. He saw the rare rose that Belle had wished for, so he picked it, only to be confronted by a hairy hideous beast that threatened to take his life. Begging to be set free, he traded a return visit, saying he would bring the lovely Belle with him in return for his freedom. The beast agreed and sent him home, along with jewels and fine dresses for the two selfish sisters. The father returned with Belle, the beauty, and she was welcomed as mistress of the castle. The beast willingly became her servant. He continually asked her to marry him, and she consistently refused, saying she only loved him as a friend. The beast let Belle return home, just for a visit, and during that time her sisters tricked her with a false show of love that encouraged Belle to break her promise of returning to the beast when she said she would. Many, many weeks passed when Belle decided to look into a magic mirror the beast had given her once as a gift. She was stunned to see a picture of him lying half dead of heartbreak near the rare rose bushes, so she used her magic ring to return to him. She wept and told him how much she loved him, and when her tears fell upon him they broke the curse placed on him many years before and he transformed into a handsome prince. They married, he promised to shave often, and they lived happily ever after.

There are several wonderful things about this fairytale:

1. She got to know him before she married him, and they were good friends before they were lovers.
2. Inner beauty was hailed throughout as more important than a sexy exterior.
3. The sacrifices they both made were rewarded.
4. Contentment brought inner riches.
5. Being faithful led to lasting love.
6. Goodness was rewarded.
7. Sometimes people don't realize they love someone until they lose them.

The decisions we make and the opinions we have, help define who we are and how we are seen. *Beauty and the Beast* were pretty nice to each other. They were caring, faithful, and committed, but they still blew it and nearly didn't last the distance. The way to not lose what you have, or end up regretting what could have been, is to firstly notice all the good things you have in front of you. Secondly, it's about being grateful, gracious, and affirming. Thirdly, it pays to not listen or hang out with selfish people who take up all your time and take you away from your love, bleed you dry, or lead you astray. And lastly, as always, it's all about how you communicate.

In relationships, communication is most likely to hit a stumbling block when we discuss loaded subjects. Loaded subjects are topics that evoke strong feelings and responses.

Anything can be up for a beastly debate. It's how we debate that makes the difference. Debating is just delivering one possibly limited perception. It's quite a different thing to pondering and contemplating. You can dispute, contest, and argue, or you can question, discuss, and maybe learn something new. Examples of topics that can be loaded:

- To shave or not to shave, money, marriage, partnership, children, parenting issues, leaving a job, beginning a job, buying a car, buying a house, adoption, pregnancy, terminations, politics, sex, sport, sexuality, rules, religion, legal requirements, insurances, race, retirement, life transitions such as birth and death, and let's not forget housework! Who does it, when do they it, how do they do or not do it?

To avoid stepping into an argument, firstly know which topics are likely to be more difficult to talk about or listen to. Then, ask open-ended questions in order to gain more information about the other person's opinions, points of view, and beliefs.

For example: I would like to have a baby before I am 35. Have you ever thought about your future in this way?

Or: I know for sure that when I die I want to be cremated. How do you feel about this subject?

Secret number 50: Love involves sharing your intention, listening with an open mind, and an open heart.

You too can have inextinguishable love like *Beauty and the Beast*. Just grow your friendship, stay interested, and aim for peaceful communication as much as you can. Maintaining peace involves keeping your critic out of the way. While you try to find what drives your beliefs, always be willing to explore other angles, view points, and information which you can then choose to process or not.

Having a gentle approach and really hearing what someone has to say in reply works great. So does allowing others plenty of time and space to respond. It's important to remember that although on one side you may be caring for your needs and opinions, on the other side he or she is being asked to explore their feelings and opinions. Somehow it's about aiming for the middle ground and being willing to exchange clear information so the discussion can continue to safely move to a place where resolution can be reached, even if that decision is to agree to disagree. It's helpful to avoid obstinate viewpoints and focus instead on interesting themes that require more research. Always be willing to increase your area of interest in things that other people believe in, and encourage them to question more thoroughly what they accept as true.

Secret number 51: Opinion is not truth.

Loaded subjects can be bothersome because they tap directly into belief systems. It helps to know why we believe what we do, and understand where our beliefs come from. We all could do with being reminded to steer clear of rehearsed performances. We need to be willing to research our ideals and query our morals and principles. Doing so allows interesting, grounded, engaging discussions. Maybe nothing is ever certain. What anyone believes is just an estimation of reality. Is it fact, fallacy or fiction? When we move away from biased viewpoints, discrimination and prejudice, and move towards tolerance, fairness and equality, pure hearts begin to shine.

- Know which topics you have difficulty conveying or receiving.
- Know where your beliefs have come from. Did they come from your parents, society, peers, something you have been taught, something you picked up from a past relationship, or something you have deemed to be so because of a past experience?
- Be willing to determine if any need re-examining, especially beliefs that are likely to contain the words always or never. (Partners always hurt me.) (You never help me.)
- Know which beliefs were formed from reactions, and which ones you have made up.

- Be willing to recognize which ones others accept or reject more readily and work out why that is so, and then explore how it affects you.

There are many things you can both do to lighten up a subject, to turn it from something ugly into something more beautiful, to create flexibility, and to understand each other's viewpoints better. You could play a game where you pick a subject, like marriage or money, and then on ten small bits of paper, each write down ten sentences about that one subject. Shuffle the answers up, and divide them out between each other. Take what you've got and condense it all into one creative sentence or poem, and read it out loud. Then swap that sentence or poem, and get the other person to condense it down to one word that he or she thinks encapsulates the essence of the subject. The idea is to make it creative and humorous, and to show that anything can be manipulated, bent, and shaped, without hurting anyone's feelings.

- Reconsider your judgements from time to time.
- Know which beliefs are based in fear, which ones are reasonable, and which may appear unreasonable.
- Recognize which of your beliefs are fixed, and which are flexible.
- It's not only appearances that can be deceiving; rigid viewpoints may be unreliable or illusory.
- How you act or react to various statements is a choice.
- Be the kind of person who believes in transformation.
- Bend a little, and believe that change is possible.

Like the tale of *Beauty and the Beast*, know that things are not always what they seem.

Love is transformative.

Humility, pureness of heart, and paying attention to the love you have brings great rewards.

The Magic Porridge Pot

Jacob and Wilhelm Grimm's fairytale *The Magic Porridge Pot* starred a dutiful young girl and her cash strapped single mother. When starvation hit, the girl went into the forest to search for food and instead came home with a little magic pot given to her by a kind old woman, who told her to say "Little pot, cook," and it would cook porridge. She was told to say "Little pot, stop" and it would stop. Finally freed from poverty and hungry tummies, the girl and her mother ate sweet porridge as often as they wanted. One day when the little girl was out, her mother asked the little pot to cook, and it did. She ate until she was full, but then realized she didn't know the magic words to make it stop cooking, so it cooked and cooked and overflowed and filled the house, and then the next house, and then the whole street, as if it wanted to satisfy the hunger of the whole world. When the little girl returned home she saved the day by saying "Little pot, stop," and it did. Everyone who had come to see what was happening then had to eat his or her way back to town.

The Magic Porridge Pot or *Sweet Porridge* as it was sometimes called, is a wonderful tale that reminds us of four important things.

1. Random acts of kindness can change your life.
2. It's important to nourish those around you.
3. Always read the instructions first, especially if the object is enchanted.
4. When you begin something, know how to manage it, and how to end it.

In relationships it also helps to know what words to use and what sort of magic they might invoke. Communicating with love, calm, and confidence, goes a long way towards satisfying the kind of hunger many people feel in relationships. Tapping into the goodness within and giving goodness to those we love, has the ability to spill over like magic porridge and create an avalanche of positive change.

One of the most successful all-important tools that anyone can learn to use in any kind of relationship is the standard who, what, when, why, and how formula. This will be explained in more detail in the next couple of pages. Asking these questions in close personal relationships can benefit everyone in exactly the same way as they do in business settings where they're more commonly used. It makes more sense to calmly ask a question and gain further information than it does to react, justify, defend, or argue.

Secret number 52: A magical thing occurs when people grasp the concept of asking less emotionally charged questions.

Magic, kindness, care, concern, and love, can spread far and wide like magic porridge. Many people end up benefiting from being asked what they think. When people nourish each other, they are more able to naturally nourish their children, families, and all the people they come into contact with in their neighbourhoods and workplaces. Kindness feeds kindness. Goodness works in much the same way as overflowing porridge or rising bread dough, it doubles and triples and contributes ripples of contentment in its wake. Just imagine if we swapped the image of an expanding sea of porridge for a tidal wave of caring, loving, compassionate, curious communication. We could have a tsunami of positive change sweeping nations.

Whenever things reach a point of not feeling quite right, or if communication becomes difficult, be willing to take responsibility and see if it's something you may have contributed to. Ask yourself:

- How am I responsible?
- What part do I have to play in this?
- Is this a direct consequence of my behaviour?
- Am I being fair?
- Did I keep my agreements?

There's also the reality that you may have done nothing to contribute to the pickle you are in. Sometimes in discussions the unfortunate reality is that people often:

- miss the mark entirely;
- project their thoughts and feelings onto you;
- act totally irrational;
- get tired and just forget to be respectful;
- could be run down, getting sick, be under-resourced; or they just
- slip up and get lazy.

Whatever the reason, it's now your job to take hold of the sweet porridge pot, brew up some nourishment and turn things around.

Secret number 53: If what you are doing isn't working, stop and do it differently.

How many couples begin communicating in a good way without knowing the magic words to guide it to a good ending? The way people talk to each other can veer into uncomfortable realms almost as though there is some kind of unwritten rule that says it's acceptable to be mean and defensive, to raise voices, to call each other names in the heat of the moment, or to use a tone that's unacceptable when we don't know what else to do. The discomfort it causes not only to the couple fighting, but anyone who has the misfortune to be within earshot, is disconcerting. How we act and behave towards those around us, affects them. How we communicate has a lot of negative or positive influence. We hold the reigns.

Staying open and endeavouring to understand is actually even more important with those we love. Why use harsh words if we don't need to? Even if someone talks to us in a way that's inappropriate, we need to keep in mind that we are always after a positive result. We're not likely to achieve peace and harmony, or even a place where we can agree to disagree, if we stoop to their level and choose to be unpleasant back. Instead:

- Stay calm and focused.
- Count to five and breathe deeply.
- Detach from emotions as much as you can.
- Speak to your beloved in the same way you would talk to a client, a colleague, or customer.
- Remove yourself from the situation if you need to.
- Watch how much easier it is to stay respectful when you take time before you speak.
- Imagine what kind of trouble you could get yourself into if you choose to lose self-control and get argumentative.

Secret number 54: Self-control is your secret weapon when responding to others.

Playing who, what, when, why, and how, is about gathering information. The aim of the game is to get others to think about what they say. The rules are simple. Your tone needs to be calm and curious. You just need to take on the naïve enquirer role and be genuinely interested in how the other person ticks. The idea is to trust that the person you are communicating with has the ability to respond in whichever way they choose. You also need to be prepared for them to walk away and not want to engage or play the game. That's his or her right.

If they do want to engage, your job is to trust their ability to empower his or herself. Your strategy is to get really good at delivering a range of who, what, when, why, and how questions, using the word *you* rather than making *I* statements. Next, you calmly listen to the information contained in their answers without pushing to be right, or trying to win. Having many combinations of possible questions on hand that you can easily choose from becomes more natural after a period of time. In the meantime, persevere.

Let's take a look at a case study from a therapy session with Cath and Amelia, to see how the who, what, when, why, and how formula works:

Cath dished out so many critical parent statements (you should, you must, you have to) to her partner Amelia that Amelia had taken to ignoring Cath. Amelia in return continually and sarcastically used statements which infuriated Cath and contributed to her pushing more.

Cath to Amelia: "You should get a proper job."

Leanne to Cath: "Breathe. Count to five and while you do, search for one of the who, what, when, why, how responses using the word *you* in it. Move away from wanting to respond from I think, I need, or I want."

Amelia to Cath: (In a mocking tone.) "Who made you the employment officer then?"

Leanne to Amelia: "Use a tone that sounds like you are really interested in what Cath is saying. Leave the emotional response out of it and try again. Your aim is to make this situation better, not worse."

Amelia to Cath: "What made you need to tell me?"

Leanne to Amelia and Cath: "Before either of you respond, Amelia, come up with more."

Amelia to Cath: "Why do you believe this?"

Leanne to Amelia: "That's good Amelia, Cath how about answering?"

Cath: "Because she never has any money."

Leanne to Amelia: "I can see steam coming out of your ears, so remember to keep things calm. Don't let her get to you. Don't be pulled into the emotion of it all. You want to know more. It's good to know more. Breathe. Detach. Go ahead and ask another curious question. Be courageous; always be willing to calmly try again with another question even when you don't get the answer you want. Amelia, I want you to come up with five responses, and Cath, just quietly take it in and listen until she is finished."

Amelia:

- "Who do you know that you could talk to about how you feel?
- What is it about me not having money that annoys you?
- When do you notice me not contributing?"
- Why does this bother you?
- How does it affect you personally?"

Leanne to Cath: "The idea of being asked questions is to encourage you to think more deeply about why you say what you say. The aim is to help you get to the underlying message, and to work out whether what you say is appropriate. More importantly it's about whether it gets you the kind of result you want. Take a breath Cath and answer one of the questions."

Cath to Amelia: "I don't like having to pay for things for you."

Leanne to Amelia: "Take it further. Ask more. Roll out as many as you can think of."

Amelia:

- "Who told you that you have to?
- What makes you feel like you have to?

- When did you notice it was a problem?
- Why do you think you need to?
- What's it like for you when you choose to pay for me?
- How does it make you feel?"

Leanne to Cath: "How is it for you Cath, when Amelia chooses to ask you a question rather than reacting, justifying, and defending?"

Cath: "It makes me think more about what I am saying. I think I blame her when in actual fact she doesn't ask me to pay for her. I just do it and I resent it, so I guess I should stop."

Leanne to Cath: "Should or could? You could stop, but do you want to?"

Cath to Leanne: "Not really, because I like to pay for some things so that I can have the pleasure of her company."

Leanne to Cath: "So you do it because you love having her around?"

Cath to Amelia: "Yes I pay for you for selfish reasons, so I will stop blaming you for not having as much money as me."

Obviously unguided it may not always go as smoothly as it did with Cath and Amelia, but it's always worth doing until you get the hang of it.

Important things to remember when asking who, what, when, why, and how questions:

- Irritation often occurs just before a breakthrough.
- Be willing to hear what his or her truth is.
- Stay patient, and keep asking until you can expose more authentic answers.
- Trust that when you communicate this way it will enhance your own life, and eventually make things easier.

When people want to tell you what you should do, say this, "How would *your* life be different if I did that?"

As good as it is to have a handful of who, what, when, why, and how questions ready to go, it's also helpful to have other responses so you don't sound like a broken record. "You should get a proper job," was Cath's original accusation. Here are some other ideas of how to answer in a way that turns down the emotional volume.

Light hearted responses:

- Wow, that's a loaded statement.
- I'll get a proper job as soon as the president calls to hire me.
- Where did that statement come from?

You could take a caring approach. Be prepared to be compassionate. Be willing to talk in a genuine, loving, and protective way. Gentle responses:

- It sounds like you need to talk to me about something difficult.
- See if you can tell me what you really need to, and I will stay quiet and listen until you have finished.

Or you could take a creative approach and get them to brainstorm solutions:

- Tell me six reasons why I might need to get a proper job.
- Add six reasons of your own to show your willingness to contribute.

"Asking the proper question is the central action of transformation in fairytales, in analysis, and in individuation. The key question causes germination of consciousness. The properly shaped question always emanates from an essential curiosity about what stands behind. Questions are the keys that cause the secret doors of the psyche to swing open."
Dr. Clarissa Pinkola Estes.

Welcome what is working and change what isn't.

The Emperors New Clothes

An emperor highly concerned with his appearance, is convinced by two charlatan tailors to have the finest suit imaginable made, from a fabric invisible to anyone who is either unfit for his position, or those too stupid to see it. The emperor recognizes fairly quickly that he cannot see the cloth, but pretends that he can for fear of appearing unfit for his position. Those close to him do the same so as to not appear stupid. The tailors supposedly dress him, and the emperor marches before his subjects who go along with the pretence, until a child blurts out that the emperor is in fact completely naked! When everyone realizes the fraud, the emperor decides to hold his head high and continue to parade with pride.

If it seems frustrating and amazing to you that no one stepped in earlier to point out the glaringly obvious fault in the emperor's plan, chances are you could be a rescuer, someone who over-functions in relationships. Sometimes stepping in and taking over can impress upon a person that you are saving, that you think they are a bit stupid and incapable of making healthy decisions for themselves. If this dynamic goes on for long enough, those who are being rescued could either get angry or unwittingly start under-functioning and begin to rely on you more and more.

Unless someone is about to be knowingly swindled, it's good to remember that most of the time everyone has the ability to get out of whatever tangle they are in, or that learning from mistakes and failures is a stepping stone to future success.

How to tell if you might be over doing it in the rescuing department:

- You feel compelled to help and heal others beyond the call of duty.
- You get exhausted from the demands placed on you.
- You feel undervalued or ripped off, and feel that others don't value your input.
- You have begun to notice people rejecting your helpful advances with an irritated overtone.

Rather than saving or rescuing, what's actually called for in an equal relationship is an adult-to-adult interaction. That's one where you ask questions that enable the other person to think for him or herself, allowing them to access their own innate wisdom. Encouraging others to work things out makes them feel more capable and intelligent. If we overly tell others what to do, it can unintentionally shift us into sounding like a parent, which can unconsciously persuade them to behave in childlike ways. The most helpful thing to remember in this instance is that partners want a partner, not a parent.

When we allow others the space to ask for our help, if and when they need it, their outcome will match their needs, which is far more empowering.

Stepping back from compulsion, and understanding what lies behind our need to be excessively concerned about others, makes room for powerful discoveries of our own. Sometimes people purposefully fantasize about what others are thinking or doing so they don't have to take a look at their own thoughts, feelings, and needs. If you think you might do this, search inside yourself and wonder who you are when you aren't fixing others.

The problem with being a rescuer is that we can inadvertently make the person we are rescuing a victim. If we highlight anyone's inadequacies often enough, it can expose vulnerability. What tends to eventually happen is the victim moves into the persecutor role and slam-dunks the rescuer, moving the rescuer into the victim position. One way to get out of what's called *The Karpman Triangle* is to step back and trust that others are capable of making their own decisions.

Think back to a time when someone told you things about yourself, in regards to what you should or shouldn't do, or how you should do it, when you didn't give the person permission to do so. Did you listen gladly and be humbly thankful? Were you automatically bursting at the seams to make the changes he or she thrust at you?

Secret number 55: Most people will make changes in their lives when they realize they need to, not when you tell them they should.

Suppress any urge to utter these types of statements:

- I think that this would be best for you.
- I can't believe you put up with this, or that.
- I think you should just...

- You should be over it by now.
- Probably anything that starts with: You should.

When we tell someone what he or she should do, or when or why they should, it is usually met with resistance, or a **yes but** answer. Yes but is a way of pushing back. People don't like to be put in a position where they have to defend or justify their decisions. We could all do with increasing our awareness and attention in regards to the kind of responses we are receiving. If a person shows any signs of distress, we needn't push harder. Yes but means it doesn't look or feel right to them. No one relishes the thought of being forced or conned by an emperor's tailor. We need to let others feel they can speak up for themselves. We can teach others that it's okay to ask us for help and advice. We could instead use statements like: If you need help from me, please just ask.

It's all about feeling comfortable enough to just listen and walk alongside others as they sift and sort through the wealth of information that they truly do have, even in the midst of whatever difficulty they might be experiencing.

Sometimes people just want to be heard, even if what they are faced with is a situation that seems insurmountable, like a huge tax debt, a job redundancy, criminal charges, a terminal illness, or a sex scandal.

It's about trusting that almost everyone is as equipped as we are to get through tough times. They might just want someone to listen or lean on, rather than someone telling them what to do.

Secret number 56: It is way better to ask, than to tell, teach, or preach.

Ask gentle questions that allow people to take action for themselves.

Helpful questions to ask:

- What is it like for you to experience this difficulty?
- Why do you think this may be happening now in your life?
- How are you feeling?
- What specifically do you need, want, or desire?

- Who else do you know that has found a way to get through this?
- Why do you think you might be having trouble with...?
- How do you think you might be able to change your situation?
- What if you came up with three ways or ideas, how would that feel?
- What do you think might have to happen?

These kinds of questions are a really safe way to support someone through a difficult time. Use the why questions very sparingly, if at all, with anyone who has been victimized. It's good to get used to asking questions without forcing them on people, or being too clinical in the way that you ask. When you ask, have genuine empathy and concern. Ask gently and kindly, with a touch of curiosity.

Times when it's okay to step in:

- If your job involves being a caregiver and you have been asked to help. Use healthy limits and boundaries, and your fail-safe recipe to empower others.
- If someone you care about is extremely depressed, stuck, or endangering themselves or others.
- If someone you know or don't know is clearly unsafe, drunk, disorientated and in a situation that requires urgent attention.
- When you are a bystander to someone who is being bullied or harmed.
- If emergency services need your assistance for something you have witnessed.
- When you have been specifically asked to help and you have boundaries in place around what is needed, when it is needed, how long it is to go on for, why it is needed, and why you are both doing it.
- Or, if someone starts parading around butt naked like the emperor and insists on being an extreme fool without realizing it, just raise your eyebrow, tap them on the shoulder and speak up sooner rather than later.

Through the Looking Glass

"I can't believe that!" said Alice.
"Can't you?" the Queen said in a pitying tone. "Try
again: draw a long breath, and shut your eyes."
Alice laughed. "There's no use trying" she said.
"One can't believe impossible things."
"I daresay you haven't had much practice," said the
Queen. "When I was your age, I always did it for
half-an-hour a day. Why, sometimes I've believed as
many as six impossible things before breakfast."
Lewis Carroll.

In *Through the Looking Glass*, nonsense and imagination run freely. There are frequent changes in time and spatial direction, including opposites and time running backwards. Mirror themes pop up amidst the craziness.

Mirrors are used to look into, and when we do, what we see is actually reflected reversed, which just like life and relationships, can be confusing.

Confusion has a purpose. It challenges the way we think. In this tale, Alice has little control over her journey once she goes down the rabbit hole. Adventuring into the unknown, Alice is thrown into chaos and confusion, and outside influences rule her more than she is able to rule herself. Being out of control is partly because she is only a child, and partly it's because Lewis Carroll purposefully created her as quite transparent. Bumbling along, in a way, reflects and represents the part of all of us that has no particular reason for anything we do. We could all benefit from doing more things for no particular reason because it's such a great way to introduce unexpected newness into our lives and relationships. Stumbling upon surprising experiences is fun and adds zest and vibrancy.

Alice does a lot of things without thinking. She appears to constantly seek compassion and understanding and yet she rarely receives it. Mostly she's just disappointed and confused. Perhaps she's just too young to realize that she has the power within to find her way back, to tip things up the right way, and to guide herself calmly and wisely, no matter how curious her journey is.

Sometimes when relationships get out of synch, we have a tendency to become overwhelmed by confusion. That's when we become tempted to throw curiosity out the window and instead exit down a rabbit hole, run, or even take substances to blank out and forget. The way to stay in a relationship when things are difficult is to simply take off your running shoes and be prepared to do whatever it takes to make things better. Do it for your own sake, and then do it because your partner deserves to be happy and fulfilled. Relationships force us to look at and heal the wounds of our past. As long as deal breakers such as extreme control, abuse, and addiction aren't present, we need to learn to hang in there and put in the effort to improve things.

> *"You come to love not by finding the perfect person,*
> *but by seeing an imperfect person perfectly."*
> **Sam Keen.**

It's an interesting and rather nice spiritual idea that we are drawn towards life partners to specifically show us what we need to learn, and that they are in our lives to help us heal and evolve. What they inadvertently do is reflect back a small part that we could do with looking at. It's good to remember that whatever irritates us the most about them, is often the very thing that we need to fix in ourselves.

In *Through the Looking Glass*, and in partnerships, chaos and drama can arrive unexpectedly, and difficulties can be magnified anytime along the journey. There are no guaranteed time frames. Resentment can even smoulder and surface for the first time, many years into a relationship.

Let's take a look at Tania and Jeff, a case study couple that have loved and lived with each other for nineteen years who had until now, experienced no serious relationship hiccups or hurdles. Their animosity came as a big surprise to them, considering they had always found ways to put amicable change in place. They had easily managed to maintain a gentle, loving and kind relationship, in good times and less good times. The shock that they felt when they found themselves being less than accommodating, and even intolerant towards each other, was akin to falling down a rabbit hole into an alternative world. Their distress at wanting

Leanne French

to throw their relationship away when they hit their very first rocky bump worried them enough to seek help. Luckily because they were so open and evolved they had a willingness to accept feedback, explore insights, and work at understanding their irritation and hurt, which luckily tipped things up the right way again, reduced confusion, invited clarity, and enabled them to stay together.

After telling them to stop the nonsense and get curious, this is what they considered, explored, and discussed that helped set them back on track:

One of the first practical things to do:

Look at time lines such as how old you might have been when a parent or loved one separated, died, became sick, or when things first changed in a major way for you. Then look at the length of time you have been with your partner. Chances are that rifts begin at exactly the same point in time. If you had to shift from your family home that you loved when you were six, it could be possible for you to get itchy feet six years into a relationship. Jeff for example, was nineteen when his mother died and it was exactly nineteen years into his relationship that he unconsciously began expecting to be abandoned. It was also when he began behaving in ways that made Tania think about leaving him.

The second practical thing to do:

Think about how you initially responded to the original wound you experienced, and bring those memories into your conscious awareness. Jeff for example identified with having been abandoned. Even if you were numb, that is a response. Don't delve too deeply or drown in the horror of old memories, just briefly dip your toes in and get the information you need and move on.

The third practical thing to do:

Become aware of how many of those original responses and ways of being you bring into the present situation. Look at whether you are choosing to cause the experience. Explore what you are hoping to achieve, and see whether it's working or not.

The fourth practical thing to do:

Absolutely quit doing things the same way and do things differently. Play with new ways of responding and behaving. Watch how drawn you are to acting out of habit. When that occurs, pull a new response out of your basket of tricks, and then enjoy watching your relationship dynamic change for the better.

The fifth practical thing to do:

Withdraw blame. If and when you find yourself focusing on his or her faults, breathe, let it go, and bring your awareness back to your own feelings and behaviours. Refuse to be irritated, selfish, or disconnected. Instead, separate how you feel from what he or she chooses to do or not do. Don't allow it to affect you, and refuse to grow the belief that they are doing it to you. Be curious about what drives you to be upset by what he or she says or does, and seek to be less affected by external events and more conscious of internal actions.

The sixth practical thing to do:

To love, love, and love some more. Through thick and thin, good and less good, and especially when things are topsy-turvy.

Secret number 57: Push yourself to notice what your beloved is doing right.

- Only seek to see goodness in each moment, hour, and day.
- Praise.
- Affirm.
- Write a list of what you love about each other and pin it up somewhere visible.
- Create a special dinner with uninterrupted time together where you only discuss fabulous memories, and watch how it draws you closer.
- Find three things about your beloved each and every day that you feel grateful for, and tell him or her.
- Know that he or she deserves to be loved and cherished as much as you do.

Humpty Dumpty Sat on the Wall

"I don't know what you mean by glory," Alice said. Humpty Dumpty smiled contemptuously. "Of course you don't, till I tell you. I meant there's a nice knockdown argument for you!" "But glory doesn't mean a nice knockdown argument," Alice objected. "When I use a word," Humpty Dumpty said, in rather a scornful tone, "it means just what I choose it to mean, neither more nor less." Lewis Carroll - Through the Looking Glass.

Most couples feel like they're in a knockdown argument when they fight in the same way, over and over. You know the kind of disagreement, the one where no one wins and everyone pushes harder to be heard and understood? Although couples insist they are hopeful of a different result each time they set out to get their way, that just doesn't come without changing the dynamic, learning to avoid the brick wall, and actually communicating differently. It doesn't matter how thick-skinned or thin-shelled you are, if you bang your head against a brick wall long enough it's eventually going to crack and hurt.

Working with couples in difficulty is often like being a strategically placed fly on the wall. Better that than a tipsy egg! Stepping back and viewing communication techniques with curiosity is the secret that invites clarity to a situation.

Secret number 58: Emotional detachment allows you to observe the roles you both play, and see patterns that persist.

You are likely to have a brick wall if:

- The fighting feels overly familiar and you feel stuck.
- Communication is scrambled and you feel unheard and misunderstood.
- Your frustration is bigger when you finish arguing, than when you began.

A lot of stuck couples say they have tried everything, when in fact it's more likely that they are just attempting to fix things the same way with a different tone, slant, or angle.

When you reach the same stuff different day moment, that's the time to change things and stop taking the fall. All the king's horses and all the king's men won't help put things back together again. It's actually up to you.

Once upon a time back in the olden days, there was an interesting healer person in each village called a shaman. A shaman was someone people went to see when they were stuck, frustrated, and needed wise counsel. What would happen is that they would line up, wait their turn, and once in the midst of the shaman's presence he or she would be asked to spill out their problem. The shaman would then ask a shockingly simple question, "What have you not yet tried?" This would allow the person to blurt out all the things they hadn't yet attempted, or were too scared to attempt. To their great dismay the shaman would then say, "So go do that" and wave him or her on their way.

I know it sounds naively simple, but if you simply stop doing something one way and try another, you will get a better result. It's a very successful technique.

So go ahead, identify your brick wall:

- Recognize and observe the stuck dynamic that you both get into.
- Dissect it by noticing what you actually do. Be aware of the kinds of things you say and how you say them, why you think you say them, what you hope to gain by saying them, and look at the result you end up with.
- Notice the feeling you are left with, and the feelings created in your beloved.
- Imagine a more ideal result.

Now take some time to think about:

- what you don't do;
- what you would never dream of doing; and
- all of the things you are too afraid to say or do.

Sometimes one option may jump out at you, followed by a slight panic and a thought that says, "There's no way I am going to do that!" That's the one to choose.

Search for a few new responses to select from the next time you find yourself in a brick wall situation. Put them in into your **basket of tricks**. Some people find it helpful to actually visualize a basket. Mine has a bunny in it. If your basket of tricks has eggs in it, make sure they are hard-boiled! Your basket of tricks can be used in many instances. Jammed situations don't just occur in love relationships they crop up in families and workplaces. Stay brave and get excited about conversing in new ways. Pull your tricks out all over the place and watch change occur.

Let's look at a case study of Jim and Mary. They have a brick wall dynamic that goes like this:

Jim orders Mary around a lot, and Mary usually gets to a point where she doesn't like it and wants him to stop.

Mary: "I am doing the best job I can. Why don't you mind your own business and leave me alone."

Jim: "If I left you alone, the dishes would never get done."

Mary: "They would so; I do them when I want to do them. Why do you always act like you are the boss of all of us?"

Jim: (now escalated) "Who else has a problem with me? I don't always do it to everybody."

Mary: "How come you can't see that you do? The boys want a father that spends time with them. They shouldn't have to come home in the holidays and build a deck for you."

Jim: "It's not for me, it's for us, and why should I have to do all the work? I pay their university fees so why can't they give something back?"

You get the general picture? Jim pushes, Mary stays passive for too long and then gets aggressive. She justifies and defends, exaggerates, verbally pushes him away, and pulls other people into the argument causing triangulation. Then Mary wonders why Jim gets harder to deal with, why the arguing seems to ignore her need to be acknowledged and valued, and turns instead into an argument about their sons.

Although Jim has many things we may think he needs to change, Mary's ways of coping are outdated so she wants to replace them with healthy new tricks.

When Mary thinks about things she never says or does, the answers come quite quickly for her. She says she:

- never makes light of what's going on;
- never walks in his shoes to understand why he might be bossy;
- never agrees with Jim; and
- absolutely would not want to ignore him.

Mary's new basket of tricks could contain:

Humour.

- You are so not the boss of me.
- Yes sir, Sergeant Major, right away sir.

Compassion.

- What can I do to help you?
- I feel for you when you are this stressed.
- Is everything okay with you? I notice that you are doing that ordering around thing that you do when you have a lot going on.

Agreement.

- You know what, you are right, I am not in the position to help you right now, and that must be hard for you.

The willingness to change.

- It seems like you want me to do more than I can for you sometimes, and I am finding that difficult.
- What do you think we could do about this?
- Do you have any ideas?

Release.

- She could take a breath and choose not to respond at all.
- She could leave talking about the dynamic until the stress levels have reduced.
- When that time comes, she could take responsibility for not speaking up clearly enough, often enough, and declare that she will be assertive rather than aggressive next time it happens.
- She could tell him that he may need to change how he asks her to do things, to get a better result. This is the one she was most afraid of doing. This will get the most results in the long run.

Play with knowing what could work in your basket of tricks. Its good to remember that:

- Even one fresh way of responding can change the dynamic.
- Testing new responses out requires a fun approach.
- The challenge it presents can be approached with enjoyment.
- Results always need celebrating.
- A successful outcome then requires you to do your very best to maintain those new ways of communicating.

"Ultimately spiritual awareness unfolds when you're flexible, when you're spontaneous, when you're detached, when you're easy on yourself and easy on others."
Deepak Chopra.

Three Billy Goats Gruff and Other Clever Stuff

Three Billy Goats Gruff is an ancient Norwegian fairytale about three goats who have no grass left to eat where they live. They need to get to a field on the other side of the river where lush grass grows. To get there they must first cross a bridge that a scary, ugly, smelly troll lives under. He has a nasty habit of eating anyone who passes by. The first to cross the bridge is the smallest goat. The troll appears and threatens to gobble him up. The little goat cleverly convinces the troll to wait for the biggest goat to come across because he is so much larger and much more gratifying as a feast. The greedy troll agrees and lets both the small and middle size goat across. When the biggest goat gets on the bridge and is accosted by the hungry troll, he is luckily so strong that he easily bunts the troll into the river with his horns, and crosses happily. From then on the bridge is safe, and all three goats are able to go and eat as much scrumptious grass as they like, whenever they like.

There's a high price to pay on your sanity when a troll begins to demand tolls. If things seem to be getting a little ugly, and you feel like someone is controlling your bridge crossings (like your decisions, your direction, your plans, your hopes, your dreams, your time, your salary, who you can be friends with, or how you parent) try approaching the difficulty like a goat.

Goats are agile, cunning, clever, and quick thinking. You don't always have to act like you are the biggest or strongest to get your way, although that usually works as a last resort. First, find intelligent ways to work out how to overcome obstacles on your path.

Keeping out of trouble:

- Stay in the present moment and embrace the chaos.
- See your hurdle as a challenge, a learning experience.
- Stay on topic. See it as a topic rather than an issue, so you can lessen your emotional attachment and therefore your emotional response.
- Take responsibility for your feelings and use I statements.
- Be realistic. Know that disagreements are a part of life.
- Be compassionate towards your partner's vulnerabilities.

- Listen to who he or she really is, not who you want them to be.
- Use wisdom.
- Answer questions that are asked.
- Be resourceful.
- Act co-operatively.
- Use social restraint.
- Be patient.
- Encourage, and do what you can to earn back respect.
- Stay optimistic.

Making more trouble:

- Only have concern for yourself.
- Bring up the past.
- Criticize.
- Hold onto bitterness and regret.
- Play: What if?
- Hack at each other's spirit.
- Control, because you feel out of control.
- Yell.
- Name call.
- Be disrespectful.
- Stay intolerant.
- Push to be right.
- Deflect.
- Blame.
- Justify and get defensive.
- Compete.

Least recommended:

- Be ruthless.
- Act selfish.
- Be unkind.
- Act like the big goat and tell the troll you'll poke their eyeballs out their ears.

Once Upon a Tangled Time

Uncle Remus was a fictional narrator from a collection of African-American folktales about the Southern States of America. (Folktales are just like fairytales except they don't usually have a magical element.) In one of his famous trickster tales titled *The Tar Baby*, Brer Fox had some revenge to inflict upon Brer Rabbit, so he made a tar baby out of tar and turpentine. Brer Rabbit was incensed at the tar baby's ability to ignore him, so he punched him and got stuck. This is best part of the tale, not because it's violent, but because there is a lesson in it that tells us that things aren't always what they seem.

The more stuck Brer Rabbit got, and the more he struggled to get out of his situation, the more tangled up he got. It's amazing how a problem can get worse the more you struggle with it. Feeling helpless, Brer Rabbit found a way to pull on his cunning, witty and persuasive self and pleaded with Brer Fox to not fling him in the briar patch, which of course prompted Brer Fox to do just that. Rabbits love briar patches (and reverse psychology) so Brer Rabbit was very happy to have made such a lucky escape.

Rather than losing his temper in the first place, which had a less than fabulous consequence, maybe Brer Rabbit could've showed restraint, shrugged his shoulders, and hopped on his merry way? How often could we benefit from showing restraint, ignoring, and letting some things go in a relationship?

Sheer frustration can lead people to do extraordinarily stupid things.

Secret number 59: If someone is baiting you to argue, don't take the hook. Swim around and find a calm, creative response rather than a reaction.

Someone's got to do it, so why not you?

Why choose to argue and make your day miserable? Think of it like this. If you were fine before he or she made a comment that riled you, then you can still choose to continue to feel fine after it. Here's how to keep your cool:

- De-personalize, detach, and slow down your response time.
- Count to five and take a breath because it allows you to access your adult thinking self rather than your reactive self.
- Don't jump to the conclusion that what's going on has to be about you.
- Stay focused on content that makes sense, and try to ignore emotional outbursts. Gently question what they have said.
- Be willing to check whether he or she is stressed or tired, and ask how you could make things better.
- Change the mood of the conversation and trick them into escaping.

Secret number 60: Stay focused on what someone says, not why you think they have said it.

People can easily make a mistake of falsely interpreting what they have heard, which can lead to trouble. Make an effort to not read more into anything than is necessary.

Secret number 61: We each have a responsibility to manage our moods and express our needs, wants, and vulnerabilities in a respectful way.

Repeat back what you think you heard him or her say, rather than:

- jumping to conclusions;
- going off on a tangent;
- getting stuck in *The Tar Baby;* or
- tangling up the lines of communication.

When you reflect back what he or she has said, they can say yes or no, until they feel that they have been heard in an unrefined way. It's about sticking to the facts and not being afraid to repeat back what you think you heard if you aren't clear.

Managing your mood also means being willing to admit if you are stuck for words. Rather than sitting, grinning, grimacing and saying nothing like *The Tar Baby* and possibly winding someone up unnecessarily, it's acceptable to say that you don't know how to answer.

Secret number 62: Most people actually want to be loved and supported but don't always know how to behave in a way to get what they want.

Most people don't intentionally set out to create conflict. A lot of times it's accidental. Brer Fox was an exception! He is the exact kind of extreme pest that drives people to want to exact revenge. As soon as we identify menacing troublemakers, we need to find ways to extract ourselves from their company and then avoid them like the plague. Once we grow the belief that we don't deserve to be victimized and we invite others to speak to us in the same respectable way that we speak to them, it becomes impossible to accept anything less.

In relationships some people actually argue to gain closeness, and some argue to create space. Others do it to be heard, and some do it to shut people up. We all have sabotage techniques without consciously meaning to. We are more likely to use old ways of communicating that don't particularly serve us when we are tired or lacking in resources. Self-care includes being responsible for getting enough rest and finding resources that enable us to cope and stay calmly assertive. You are in control of how you live your life, which is why it's vital to make room for rest and recreation. Refuse to run on empty. Fill your tank with nourishing fuel.

Secret number 63: Be compassionate. That means being understanding, sympathetic, tender, concerned, curious, warm, and loving.

If you are ever faced with what seems to be an insurmountable problem, the best tool to use is compassion. Negative emotions are easier to grab at if you feel threatened. It may seem easier to poke; to be righteous, stubborn, unforgiving, or revengeful, but that kind of approach has no long-term gain. If you can, take a breath, step back, and seek to understand the hidden gift behind the difficult situation you are in. You don't have to display saintly patience, or show the same amount of compassion as Mother Teresa, just be willing to try a new approach and learn to step back from chaos and drama.

Who's Afraid of the Big Bad Wolf?

A mother pig sent her *Three Little Pigs* out into the world to seek their fortune and said, "Whatever you do, do it the best that you can, because that's the way to get along in the world." The first little pig obviously wasn't that good at listening. He built his house the easy way, out of straw, and in no time at all a very hungry big bad wolf came along and blew it down. The little pig ran squealing to his marginally less lazy brother's house of sticks. The salivating wolf, excited at the thought of gobbling up two little pigs in one mouthful, had no trouble blowing the stick house down. The two little pigs then dashed over to the sensible third brother's brick house, which was so strong that the wolf couldn't blow it down no matter how hard he tried. The wolf did everything he could to entice and trick the pigs out of their house, and they continued to outsmart him. Not being one to give up or back down, the wolf decided to enter the brick house down the chimney. Down he went, falling straight into a pot of boiling water that purposefully lay in wait for him, and the pigs ate him all up (even though they aren't supposed to eat meat) and they lived happily ever after.

Most of us can probably hear the distant echo of our own mother's cautionary voice, telling us, "If a job's worth doing it's worth doing properly." This tale proves it's true! In relationships, thinking ahead, being aware of possible consequences and knowing what's needed to protect ourselves from strong or powerful people who will pop up from time to time to oppose or deceive us, is a very good plan. We ought to remain hopeful that we can be victorious, and believe that our hard work rather than our desire for instant gratification can bring successful results. It's also quite fun to creatively image what kind of house the three piggy brothers could have built had they banded together and combined their skills.

So, after a late night or a tiring, stressful day when grumpiness sets in, who doesn't need reminding to not huff and puff and blow the house down? The ultimate aim is to create peace and keep that roof over your head!

There are definite times to manage our wolf-like behaviours, such as:

- not persistently going after things we can't or shouldn't have; and
- knowing when to back off from an argument that's too heated.

Just imagining a wolf and a pig in each other's vicinity conjures up a picture of trouble, and yet it's not that uncommon for completely contrasting types of personalities to hold a certain allure. Many opposites fall in love and share brick houses. Under stress or undue pressure, a lot of us wish their beloved would handle things in the same manner as we do, and somehow magically meet our unspoken needs. When personalities oppose, so can reactions and responses. When someone doesn't do it the way we do, feelings can get hurt, and more often than not anger surfaces. When tempers flare, you can be sure that your style of trying to resolve things is likely to be opposite too.

If one of you is more outwardly focused, (wolf-like) expressive, and quick to respond with a tendency to want to control things when they don't go the way you would like them to, you could be the type to boil over or blow like a volcano. Explosions may subside quickly, but you can leave others flailing around in the aftershock and embers which is less than ideal.

If one of you is more inwardly focused, quiet, slower to process, more stubborn, (pig-like) with a tendency to sulk and withdraw when things don't go your way, your anger is likely to be slow to rise. This style can feel punishing to others especially if it's left unattended and smoulders on for ages.

Both styles have manipulative tendencies and don't resolve conflict. In the *Three Little Pigs*, being smart is a good thing. Welcoming a sense of calm into your relationship takes being smart and finding a new action plan.

What to do differently if you are the withdrawing, passive type:

- simply stay in there and stay connected;
- participate;
- speak up and be heard;
- even if you know it won't change what's happening, do it anyway;
- honor who you are;
- stand up for yourself;
- trust in the process of speaking out;
- ask to be spoken to in a respectful and gentle way;
- be courageous and don't go giving up before you have even begun;
- don't believe that every interaction will end in doom and gloom;

- know that when you choose to shut down, it only exacerbates the problem and invites in the very same anger you are busy trying to avoid; and
- keep your body language open and your mood light.

What to do differently if you are an aggressive type:

- be calm and breathe deeply;
- push your palms down on a hard surface and count to ten;
- be curious and don't think that you have all the answers;
- say what you want gently, respectfully, and with less force;
- consider the consequences of what you say and how you say it, before you say it;
- think about being more real and express your vulnerability rather than your anger;
- aim for a rational response rather than a super-charged emotional response; and
- sift and sort and learn to let some things go.

For both styles:

- laugh more;
- play with new ways of communicating until a better one clicks into place;
- focus on the positive aspects of having opposing personalities; and
- continue to see the good in each other rather than being critical.

Secret number 64: Gradually adopt some of your partner's qualities that feel very different to yours, and remember why you fell in love in the first place.

What we love about someone is often the very first thing that will annoy us about him or her. Annoyance disappears when we can instead adopt that quality. Quietness for example, can bring more calm into a socially focused hectic life, and a life in need of more stimulation could benefit from adopting outgoing, charismatic qualities. Those closest to us have much to teach us when we are willing to learn.

I'll Huff and I'll Puff and I'll Blow Your House In

Not by the hair on my chinny-chin-chin!

Learning to be compassionate when anger is present can be fraught with confusion. A lot of people have trouble working out whether they are allowed to get angry towards other people, or not. Part of the confusion is working out whether we are supposed to just turn the other cheek, or whether ignoring other people's anger allows them to be bullies. Thankfully there is balance to be had. Even the Dalai Llama notices anger. He watches it come and he watches it go! Being compassionate, having less attachment, remembering that huffy puffy wolves have a right to be happy too, and dealing with anger rather than letting it gobble up our inner peace, is a good thing to aim for.

If we don't get the opportunity to huff and puff now and again, chances are we could explode when we least expect it. No matter how many tools are available to facilitate calm communication, some people will never use them. Others who thrive on anger could just be inherently bad, messed up, or dangerous. A healthy expression of anger however, actually has a purpose, a very, very good purpose.

Secret number 65: Anger is a motivator for change and transformation, and needs to be used appropriately.

Anger is an acceptable emotion that needs expression, just like joy or sadness or happiness. Getting in touch with our right to be angry is a part of healthy development. Hopefully you won't have to angrily stand up for your rights very often in your relationship (or bust houses down) but anger management is included here because if you incessantly struggle with anger issues with family, friends, workmates, or even strangers, it can turn a good relationship sour over time. Outside influences can change moods, and if your mood is dark or distant a little too often, it could make you hard to live with.

There are two types of anger: Anger from the past and anger in the present.

If for example, you are faced with words and actions that step over your boundaries, intimidate or threaten you in some way, that's the one to get angry about as it occurs. Deal with it in the *present*. Don't let it fester, don't harbour a grudge, and don't save it up for another time. Tell yourself that getting to a place of peace benefits you, and step forward bravely.

Secret number 66: Being angry in the present is a way of standing up for yourself and ensuring that whatever is happening to you, doesn't happen again.

It's all a part of teaching others how to treat us. We need to be able to protect ourselves and make it clear that inappropriate behaviour is uncalled for. If you deal with each and every situation that presents itself to you, when it presents itself to you, you will be clear and current with your anger.

Expressing anger carried over from your *past* is important. It's a healing way to clear your slate and reduce residue. Most people can recall situations where they didn't get a chance to deal with something they wished they could have. Chances often get missed because either it felt unsafe, or it simply wasn't appropriate at the time. The release of past anger is private. You don't have to actually face up to people from the past or confront demons and dragons head on. If you decide to consciously undertake anger exercises, just remember to do them safely without hurting or harming yourself, others, or property.

See the following list for appropriate and effective ways to rid anger from your body so that you can begin to leave it behind you, and not drag resentment (which is just anger sent again) into future situations. You may find it a bit forced or strange to begin with, but once you give yourself full permission to let rip, and let it out in big huffs and puffs, you can release an enormous amount of pressure from your mind and body.

Things you can do to verbally release anger from the past:

- Yell, scream, or curse into your pillow as loudly as you can. Pillows muffle noise amazingly well. Try it right now. Pick up a pillow or cushion and scream into it.

- Let everything out loudly, under the water, in a bath, or in a swimming pool. No one can hear. It's tried and tested.
- Beat your tightly closed fists into a soft, safe, spongy bed.
- Polish furniture.
- Weed a garden.
- Iron a huge stack of clothes, fast, furiously, and preferably on steam.
- Go kick a football.
- Do a serious workout.
- Wash every inch of your vehicle.
- Go to a wild windy beach and throw stones into the water.
- Kick at the sand or dirt.
- Go walking at a determined pace with your hands closed, thumbs out, looking straight ahead, and preferably move at a rate where you perspire.
- Hand-wash clothes and delight in wringing them dry.
- Tear a stack of paper or cardboard.
- Make and burn a controlled and permitted bonfire. Fire is a powerful symbol of transformation.
- Stomp on piles of rubbish, weeds, or cardboard boxes.
- Throw a private tantrum: Stomp, pound the ground, make loud noises, jump up and down, and generally behave like a toddler.
- Drive a go-kart as aggressively as you can.
- Write furiously. Write every word and feeling that you can, then rip it up into millions of pieces, or tear it up and burn it.

If your anger is very old and specifically targeted at a person who hurt or abused you:

- It may be a good idea to be guided by an expert facilitator in a cathartic group situation specifically designed to release anger.
- If you know you can manage releasing anger by yourself, you could pretend the object of your anger is a scarecrow and burn them on a bonfire.
- You could paint a figure that represents that person on a cardboard box, and smash it and stamp on it until it holds no power.
- You could throw darts at a photograph until the holes make the person disappear.

Fantastically powerful things to do to acknowledge your anger:

- On a very big strong sheet of paper, draw out your anger using black and red crayons.
- Paint it out, using big brushes and big strokes.
- Buy some sculpting medium and make yourself an angry monster that you can bake in an oven.

Surrender to your rage and allow yourself to be over the top. Get loud and scary and go a bit wild until you release what you have been carrying around all these years.

Please note:

Most of these exercises are designed for people who have trouble being angry or have difficulty believing it's okay to be angry. This advice is aimed more at people who perhaps hide behind smiles and think that being angry isn't nice.

If you know you have an anger problem where you could hurt others, or feel like you have violent tendencies, seek help without being ashamed. Get the tools that you need so you can express what you need, healthily.

Ask your health specialist for a recommendation. Search the web or local newspapers for experts, courses, or help lines.

There are many programmes specifically aimed at anger management, safe and effective parenting, and anger change. They can offer tools, wisdom and understanding, and respectfully guide you in your recovery.

Someone's Been Sleeping in My Bed

In fairytales, characters that play out courtships are generally single. I'm pretty certain there were no married women lining up to try on the glass slipper in *Cinderella*. Fairytales usually reflect good moral choices. Emotional infidelity, sexual affairs, and rampant behaviour with anyone that isn't your beloved, is wrong. It's really that simple. All three could do with being seen as forbidden and deemed to be unacceptable by more people. Selfish acts that shatter trust, cause rage, and have the ability to inflict devastating hurt, are never acceptable. People on the receiving end of betrayal often say they feel like their self-esteem has been smacked over with a baseball bat.

Because infidelity is sadly overexposed in movies, in the media, on television, (especially reality television) it has had the unfortunate effect of normalizing something that shouldn't be considered normal. It's not an acceptable way to behave. Why not just leave if you can't or won't fix what's wrong? If you know you are truly not happy, end it nicely. It's also good to let a little bit of time pass after you leave, before you get with someone else.

If you want to be set straight, the guy to read is Frank Pittman, author of a number of books including *Private Lies: Infidelity and the Betrayal of Intimacy*. He is a straight talking psychiatrist who shares extremely strong opinions in regards to keeping your union safe, sacred, and respectful. He was shocked to discover early on in his practise how many people trivialize what they do. Many of his patients who had affairs had a good sex life, but were in marriages where there was little or no intimacy. He says, "People seek affairs to have a buddy rather than to have good sex." Frank Pittman also says:

> "Any gender-based generalization is both irritating and inaccurate, but some behaviours are typical. Men tend to attach too little significance to affairs, ignoring their horrifying power to disorient and disrupt lives, while women tend to attach too much significance, assuming that the emotions are so powerful they must be 'real' and therefore concrete, permanent and stable enough to risk a life for."

In the *Dance of Deception*, author Harriet G. Lerner perfectly summarizes Frank Pittman's explanation of affairs. She says:

"In his book *Private Lies*, the family therapist Frank Pittman notes that it is the secrecy more than the sexiness in an affair that creates distance and disorientation in a marriage or primary partnership. The secrecy also helps make the lover a more emotionally compelling partner than the spouse. Typically, the lover knows all about the spouse, while the spouse knows nothing for certain. The sharing of facts and feelings can be relatively free and uncensored with the lover, while the opposite is true with the spouse."

She goes on to say:

"Thus, the very way the three players are positioned in this triangle keeps the spouse in an outside and increasingly distant position. Pittman's advice to men who have fallen in love with the other woman is: Bare in mind that a man feels closest to whichever woman shares his secrets. And, he feels uncomfortable around anyone to whom he's lying."

My favourite quote of Frank Pittman's is: "See what happens when you tell your wife the truth and start lying to the other woman."

Secret number 67: If what you are writing, saying, or doing with someone else was seen or heard by your partner, would you still do it?

If you don't think your behaviour is acceptable, or you aren't sure, then don't do it. Don't send the text. Don't send the email. Don't speak in that way on the phone to them. Don't flirt. Flirting is an effective tool for single people because it works. It nearly always leads to something more. Refuse to be suggestive. To begin backing out, think about implementing ways to spend a lot less time together.

Many clients say that their betrayal was accidental. They say they loved who they were with, they just didn't expect to feel such emotional intensity when an outsider showed them attention and affection. It's sad that they allowed themselves to feel so empty in the first place, that they didn't seek to improve themselves, and they didn't know to increase the friendship and fun with their partners. People who have accidents are commonly not paying enough attention.

Secret number 68: Misplaced politeness can lead to accidental infidelity.

If you think it's rude to say no to a flirting stranger or a colleague's inappropriate advances, how about considering why. Why would you even begin to believe you couldn't be impolite to them? Even if you can't see that they are flirting, if they are dominating your time, or overly flattering you, that's the time to change the subject, move away, and get on with something else. By not standing up for yourself and setting appropriate boundaries, you are being extremely rude to your partner. If your partner tells you they feel uncomfortable around someone, believe them. Don't argue with them, care that they feel uncomfortable.

Lots of people think they have to lie to escape disapproval. They usually say they don't let on that someone was talking to them again because their partner would only get mad. The bottom line is to not be inappropriate in the first place, or allow anyone else to talk, or behave in an inappropriate way with you. Appropriate respectful behaviour never invites rage and devastation.

Rules are there for a reason, to guide behaviour. Just because the three bears forgot to lock their house doesn't mean it was okay for *Goldilocks* to rock on in. Just because the beds looked inviting, didn't mean she had to lie down in them. Even if someone gets nude in front of you, you can look, but it doesn't mean you should ever touch. Ask them to cover up, or move away! Breaking rules shows a lack of love and regard for your partner.

- What subjects do you think are acceptable to talk about with other people?
- Which aren't?
- Is it okay for someone to pay you constant attention and ignore your partner?
- What's going on with their body language?
- Do they talk about subjects that shock you a little?
- What's happening for you when you choose to engage, rather than walk away?

People most at risk for misplaced politeness are those who partake in a lot of alcohol or drugs, those who travel away from home, people who aren't hit on that frequently, and those who perhaps don't feel attractive or confident enough in themselves. Other likely at risk scenarios include people whose friends are unfaithful, those who are in a corporate culture who accept betrayal as the norm, (especially at places like conferences) and people who don't feel secure or good enough.

Binge drinking can commonly lead to drunken chance encounters. That's the reality. Temptation is everywhere. People are capable of becoming attracted to someone else. This increases when ones guard is down or when senses are blurred. Responsibility often flies out the window with alcohol or drugs on board.

If you find yourself sharing too much time with a work colleague, meeting them everyday for coffee, telling them more than you tell your spouse, it could mean you've begun to head in the wrong direction. Here are five things that could help:

1. Step away from ticking time bombs.
2. Mix with different people.
3. Decrease the intensity of your interactions.
4. Tell whoever you are spending too much time with that you don't feel comfortable, that you are changing your behaviour, and that you would like him or her to respect your decision.
5. Check the intimacy temperature a little more often. Are your interactions too hot, too cold, or just right?

Goldilocks was bored or she wouldn't have gone looking for excitement. If you find yourself bored, sad, or flat, and feel like you need to change something, change something sensible, like how you feel. Don't throw your relationship away in order to perk yourself up. Instant gratification rarely lasts.

Beware of people who:

- overly agree with you;
- need rescuing; or
- bond with you too strongly, too soon, because he or she says they can't believe how amazing it is that they have something in common with you.

It's dismal to seek a quick romantic thrill or to think that a tense, exciting, or illicit exchange will relieve you of underlying difficulties. Secrets enliven us in a false way. That kind of excitement isn't real or long lasting.

Emotionally over-bonding with someone, too much pornography, cyber sex, and virtual sex are all about escaping real life and are best avoided.

It's so much better to be in charge of how you think, feel, and behave. Being in touch with yourself enables you to be fully present in your important relationships.

If you keep attracting people to you, or are attracted to others, there's a good chance that what you are looking for is an emotional bond, a person to have fun with. This is the exact area to work on in your relationship. That's where you need to get it.

Secret number 69: Betrayal will not reduce whatever anxiety previously existed. It will increase it.

Those who choose to step on the slippery slope of betrayal don't necessarily automatically make their lives better. This is partly because anxiety heightens reactivity. The harder we try to cover things up, the shorter our tempers get, and the more we tend to blame our partners for what they are doing and saying, instead of looking at what we might be doing to cause the problem.

Those who lie usually get punished. No wonder so much effort goes into avoiding being caught! Covering deception takes a great deal of effort. Inventing new strategies while all the time nervously covering lies, working out what information you can and can't share, gobbles up endless amounts of energy. Being guarded is a horrible way to live. It's not uncommon for our bodies to get sick and take the brunt of the strain it's put under, if pretence, self-deception, and lying goes on for too long.

Being on the receiving end of a lie can shatter all of the rules that loved ones think are in place. Those who do the betraying put their safety and security on the line.

Consider the consequences of getting caught:

- You might have to give up your job.
- You may lose your house and finances.
- You might lose your friends.
- Your children might take sides or lose respect in you.

- The stability you once knew may disappear.
- The questions fired at you may be relentless.
- The medical tests can be invasive.
- The initial cloak of shame is likely to be enormous.

Thirteen ways to avoid the slippery slope of betrayal:

1. Don't blame or look for the fault within your relationship.
2. Find ways to be happy with what you have.
3. Take responsibility for what you are doing, or not doing.
4. Curb your impulses.
5. Stay alert to temptation.
6. Identify situations that are possibly unsafe for you.
7. Learn what you can do if you are faced with a situation that isn't acceptable.
8. Have a strategy, a game plan.
9. Promise to talk about small emotional attractions and fantasies before they ever become lustful.
10. Know that you are responsible for meeting your own needs.
11. Find new ways to feel stimulated and express wild behaviour.
12. Work on deepening communication within your relationship.
13. Self-disclosure and sharing can bring you closer to your beloved.

If someone you know is behaving inappropriately:

- tell them it's not acceptable and persuade them to want to change;
- ask that they not include you in any lies;
- give them a time frame to either change their behaviour or tell their partner; and if they continue to behave badly
- be a hero and tell, even if you have to do it anonymously.

If You Step on a Crack, You Marry a Rat

The Coachman Rat was a spin off from the original *Cinderella* fairytale. The tale was about Robert the rat, a rat that was transformed into a coachman, then back into a rat (that still spoke like a human) at the stroke of midnight. Robert desperately wanted to be a permanent human so he undertook a mammoth search for a fairy godmother to make his wish come true.

Most rats aren't like Robert. For a start they aren't part human! Most rats are not the marrying kind. They make amazing pets with their cute little hands and long tails, but a marriage with a rat in it is a guaranteed recipe for disaster.

A common question after betrayal is identified is: Can trust be rebuilt? A typical answer is: It depends on so many factors. Were you the rat that did the hurting, or did you get hurt? Do you want help to change your behaviour, or relieve your guilt?

Luckily, most things including trust can be healed if you are willing to work at it. Getting help for ratty behaviour requires that you spend time looking at healing any damage you may have caused. If your partner finds out, or if you wish to confess, the same rule applies. Your partner is not at fault, and he or she is not there to help you feel better. If you desire to stay together, your job is to help them feel better and you have to keep making them feel better until they believe in you again.

Secret number 70: If you want to be trusted, you have to behave in a trustworthy way.

If you are a repeat offender, a philanderer, the kind of person who has had many affairs, chances are you are an angry person who doesn't believe in equality. If you have chosen to repeatedly assert your power, and if have consistently hurt, devalued, degraded, and thrown love away, then real relationships must be too demanding for you. The kind of work you might need to do is to understand why you are filled with fear and insecurity. Rebuilding trust will be the least of your worries. A vow of celibacy, rat bait, or a dog zapper collar might help you, but let's face it; you probably aren't likely to be reading this book in the first place.

If you have emotionally betrayed someone and you're having trouble changing your behaviour, you could do with confessing.

If on the other hand you are capable of change, have managed to recognize that what you did was wrong, were able to realize your ratty behaviour before any damage was done, and you have learnt from it, be thankful, move on, and never do it again. Consider yourself told off.

Look at what you do, and what you choose not to do. Do you withhold affection or shut down a lot? Are you contributing to a healthy relationship, or not?

Whether you confess, or are caught, the truth can be painful. It can also be immensely empowering. What it can do, is highlight where the cracks are and bring to light improvements that could be made.

Expect anger rather than be shocked by it.

Emotional betrayal shatters all the rules that your beloved thinks were in place. It can make them wonder what else is a lie.

Secret number 71: Those who have nothing to hide; hide nothing.

A helpful rule of thumb is to never tell anyone they should be over it. It's normal:

- for others to struggle with what you have done;
- to not trust you;
- to expect big changes from you;
- for you to have to check in with your partner many times to prove that you are where you say you are, doing what you are supposed to be doing;
- to be expected to do whatever he or she needs you to do, to help them get past it; and
- for you to have to apologize and begin to work towards healing the pain you may have caused.

Ask yourself every day: What am I doing to help them get over it?

Secret number 72: Attraction is often just a distraction, a way of avoiding a deeper unacknowledged emotional issue that you have.

Lust and sex can be addictive. They can anaesthetize feelings and completely distract you from any pain and underlying issues that may need healing.

Attractions kept secret are more likely to be acted on because secrecy increases excitement.

- Blow the secret.
- Being afraid of what you could do, rather than actually doing it, rapidly brings you back into relationship with your partner.
- Telling shifts you out of an inappropriate friendship/fantasy with the person you may be attracted to.

The act of telling may also bring you closer to understanding yourself, and can bring you closer to each other.

- Concentrate on healing your issue.
- Work on deepening your communication with each other.

If you are the one who has damaged the relationship, make sure that you really listen to your beloved even if what he or she has to say feels hurtful or difficult. They need to know that you understand the consequences of your actions, and they may need you to hear how your actions have impacted them.

- Do whatever it takes until your partner can find emotional peace.
- Promise to double-check your appropriateness.

Together you could:

- Recognize any distance that was present before your attraction.
- Talk about how much attention you previously paid to your partner.
- Tell him or her what you are afraid of.
- Remember that even if a relationship had no distance, temptation is something anyone can be exposed to.
- Never take each other for granted.
- Look at how you both manage anxiety and emotional intensity.
- Set new boundaries.

- Come up with safety action plans.
- Talk safely about your wants and needs without pressuring each other.
- Bring the fun back.

If you are married and you have children, you have an obligation and a commitment that needs consideration.

Whether trust can be rebuilt when you have actually had sex with someone else is something harder to advise. That's a complicated issue. Telling is highly dependant on whether it could destroy your partner. Some people can cope and some can't.

It's important to confess if you have been a dirty rat and had unsafe sex, because you've not only put your partner in emotional danger, but physical danger. Lives could be at risk. If you suspect that your beloved has been unfaithful and they refuse to tell you any details, go to your medical centre and ask to get some tests run. It's always better to be safe than sorry.

- How you tell the truth always makes a difference.
- Telling the truth in the presence of a therapist can reduce reactivity and resistance.
- If either of you is likely to not respond or react in a healthy, or safe way, seek help.

"Living with integrity means: Not settling for less than what you know you deserve in your relationships. Asking for what you want and need from others. Speaking your truth, even though it might create conflict or tension. Behaving in ways that are in harmony with your personal values. Making choices based on what you believe, and not what others believe."
Barbara De Angelis.

How to Undo Cruel Spells

In fairytales the culprit who casts cruel spells and does whatever it takes to make someone's life miserable, usually comes in the form of a wicked witch, a black-hearted queen, or an evil sorceress. In real life, betraying and lying to those who trust us comes pretty close.

If you need to make amends for cunning, cruel, or malicious behaviour, all hope is not lost. Follow the format below and know that in order to heal a grievance you'll need to do whatever it takes to stay away from justifying, defending, minimizing, or arguing your point. Stay away from advising anyone to get over it, or behaving in any way that shuts down their hurt feelings. People have a tendency to over explain themselves when they attempt to shift blame. Know that when you are in the wrong, others have every reason to be reactive, hurt, and angry.

Here are the seven steps to begin to make it better:

1. Be clear about what you did wrong. (I emotionally bonded with another person and it was wrong of me.)
2. Own up to what you did with no excuses. (I didn't choose to think before I acted and I behaved selfishly hoping to get my needs met, whilst blatantly ignoring yours.)
3. Be willing to admit that your wrong-doing hurt him or her in the process. (It was inexcusable and selfish of me and extremely hurtful to you.)
4. Say sorry and mean it. (I am so sorry for behaving in this way.)
5. Ask what you could do to begin to make things better. (Please tell me some of the things you might need in order to trust me again? What do you need me to do to help heal what I have done?)
6. Name one or two things that you will actually do, to not do it again. (I have deleted him or her from my contacts list and have clearly communicated that it will never happen again. I have changed my place of employment to remove myself from the situation.)
7. Together, come up with creative, sensible solutions that you will put in place in the future to avoid violating trust ever again.

- I will only share my intimate thoughts and feelings with you.
- I will be honest and honour you as my partner.
- Because I love you, I will behave respectfully and only say and do things in the company of others that you would consider safe.
- I will never allow this to happen again.
- I will get help for myself from an expert.
- I promise to take the advice from an expert and do everything I can to attend and participate until I find the reasons why I behaved like I did, and learn to not ever hurt you again.
- I will admit to and fix my drinking problem.
- Or, I will admit to and fix my drug problem.
- Or I will attend SLAA meetings. (Sex and love addicts anonymous.)
- Or I will not drink any alcohol in situations where you aren't present.
- I promise to check in with you everyday and share the kinds of feelings that I should have been sharing with you in the first place.
- I will make every effort to slot back into date nights with you, gently taking it at your pace to reconnect with you.

*"Replace fear-based thinking with love-based thinking.
Every time you're making a choice, ask yourself if
it's going to cultivate the experience of unity and love
or the experience of separation and stress."
Deepak Chopra.*

Mistakes are an opportunity to change. Change brings new possibilities.

Part
FOUR

Love
laughter
and happily
ever after

Gingerbread Walls and Peppermint Windows

There's an immediate sense of wonder when a fairytale begins as to how it will end. Rushing to the end however would only ruin the surprise. It also rules out the important, deeper, personal connection to the parts of the tale that allow us to tap into our unconscious, the same parts that reflect our psychological dynamics.

Skipping the meaningful stuff, the intrigue, the magic and the wonder, the tension of overcoming conflict, the realization and redemption, and the deserved lasting rewards would clearly spoil the excitement.

When my beloved king was asked the question: What makes things last? His immediate reply was in building terms. The word he used was tanalized. He then said, "Make sure what goes in the ground is treated, use the right materials, and if it's a roof you're talking about, make sure it's powder coated, and it should last the long haul." His correlation was spot on.

- There's a distinct link between building, fairytales, and relationships.
- In all three, truth prevails over dishonesty, generosity is eventually rewarded, and hard work generally overcomes obstacles.

With building projects, boundaries need to be defined and foundations require strengthening. Robust renovations, especially on crumbling castles calls for creative thoughts in order to get a great end result, and questions need to be asked about how the magnificent building will be maintained. They are all matters of importance. Most local council laws require that building materials last for fifty years, so in a relationship it makes sense to aim for as happily as ever after as you can possibly envisage. After all, what good is anything if it's not cared for appropriately?

Whether it's a tale to be told, a renovation project, or a loving relationship, why begin, if tragedy rather than triumph is expected?

All that we need to do is ask: What do I have to do to make sure we last the distance?

One of the most effective ways to increase a property investment is to look after what we have. We improve the grounds, pay constant attention to upkeep, landscape, and beautify. In our relationships, it's much the same. We can make what we have great by taking care of it, mostly with love, respect, and kindness. Individually it's about keeping our self-care levels up, exuding a sense of mystery and continually pursuing our own passions. Jointly it's about creating joy, having many things to look forward to, sharing common dreams, being adventurous, seeking to keep love as alive as it can be, and always moving forward together.

The beloved king's answer sits nicely alongside my own: Lots of fun. Fun is vital, yet his insights are a reminder that a cottage made of sweet things, in a forest full of hungry critters, isn't exactly going to last the distance.

Hansel and Gretel is a fairytale about a young brother and sister, cruelly abandoned by their parents during a famine, who stumble across a child-eating witch living deep within a forest in a house constructed of cake and confectionery. The two children cleverly manage to save their lives by outwitting her. The witch, the one who held *Hansel and Gretel* captive, was highly inventive and obviously knew how to entice, but she wasn't overly concerned with the maintenance side of things. How durable would peppermint windows actually be in the rain? It was obvious she was aiming for tantalizing as a theme, rather than tanalizing. If the witch had chemically treated her cottage we know it wouldn't have tasted as good, but it sure would have preserved it for historical significance. Imagine the ticket sales to that tour! Also, one has to ask how senseless it was to have a roaring fire going when the walls were made of gingerbread and cakes. What was she thinking! Besides the fact that she needed help for her cannibalistic ways, the witch could have found lasting companions if she were more familiar with consideration and compassion, admiration and adoration, and just for good measure, found some time to play along the way.

Relationship success is about unleashing our imagination and being willing to step out of routine and sameness, so part four is fun. It's all about maintaining love, laughter, and happily ever after. It's full of inspiration, encouragement, and creative ways to connect. The following pages are bursting with romantic reminders. They contain harebrained schemes and ideas. (And possibly contain traces of where a nut has been.) They offer you succulent sustenance and are guaranteed to keep your passionate sparks flickering and fan the flames of love.

Empathy is Enchanting

"Lots of people want to ride with you in the limo,
but what you want is someone who will take the
bus with you when the limo breaks down."
Oprah Winfrey.

Empathy is the capacity to recognize feelings that are being experienced by another, with accurateness and openness.

Being open and supportive naturally deepens emotional intimacy and increases feelings of satisfaction in our relationships.

Viewing everyone with the least amount of judgement and criticism possible, and with more curiosity and care, deepens our engagement to each other. It goes a long way towards creating safety and encouraging openness.

Secret number 73: When empathy is present, compassion can be felt.

Showing compassion and expressing genuine concern for the state of another is really just another way of declaring we simply wish to see them happy. We all need somebody to lean on, to support us, to cheer us on and to validate our feelings. When you have someone caring enough to help you avoid potholes yet encouraging enough to splash in puddles with you, you know they have the balance right.

Secret number 74: Step outside of yourself from time to time, take a moment to consider your loved one's views, and let them know you understand.

In friendship and love, these things help make relationships thrive:

- sharing and caring;
- banding together;
- switching perspectives;

- being willing to try to understand another's viewpoint;
- stepping into their shoes; and
- being sensitive to their perceptions.

It may feel strange but next time you come up against resistance, try pleading your beloved's case and see how it feels to pretend to be them.

Doing things together is another opportunity to deepen connections and enrich experiences, and has an added benefit of getting a chore done in half the time. Even sharing simple tasks such as doing the dishes, gardening, tidying the garage, spring cleaning, washing the house, or cleaning the windows, are invitations to be intimate and supportive.

New experiences are helpful in that they encourage us to explore different aspects of our personalities, beliefs and values, and they invite us to view and imagine how our loved ones manage the same new experiences. When we enter into experiences with openness and sensitivity the emotional atmosphere takes on a positive air. Enjoy working alongside each other in an uplifting way because it not only adds richness to the task, it helps time pass more quickly.

- In order to keep things upbeat, choose to talk about heavy-duty issues less, and light fluffy things more.
- Make your connection more about quality, rather than quantity.
- Be present, outwardly focused, and make time to bond.

Secret number 75: Be the kind of person you would want to hang out with.

- Smile.
- Laugh.
- Be loving and loveable.
- Be happy.
- Aim to be practical and productive.
- Contribute in optimistic, constructive ways.
- Have plenty of picnics, parties, and popcorn.

Dangerous and Daring Adventures

Every grown-up has a kid inside that loves to come out and play. Creating a thrilling, exquisite, lasting relationship is less about serious formulas and practical guidelines, and more about simplicity and silliness. It's all about being willing to take part in dangerous and daring adventures while our bodies are able and our spirits are willing.

Imagine sitting on a rocking chair when you are older and telling your grandchildren or nieces and nephews about the time you and your beloved sat in a shelter with your pet sheep, drinking hot chocolate in a storm because it was more fun and exciting watching the lightning from there. Or what about the time you stripped down to your undies and crossed a river in the middle of winter only to look back and find that your darling was yelling he couldn't do it, and then having to go back again only to do what he wanted once your toes thawed; run across a train bridge! Then imagine not being able to find any stories to share that made you daring and dangerous. What if all you had to share were stories about normal boring days and television programmes you watched most evenings? Television can be fraught with danger; it's just not your own. It somehow doesn't compare.

- Aim to live fully so that you'll have many sensational stories to tell.
- Captivate your audience, fill them will interest.

Recreate the thrills from fairytales:

- journey down irresistible paths;
- go in search of great riches;
- have mystical meetings with wild animals;
- really let your hair down;
- grant wishes;
- search for genie lamps;
- make mischief; and
- seek out adventures that you both dread and dream about.

Great tales are rarely filled with pastimes like complaining about people, expressing annoyance at the weather, or being irritated by traffic. Creating memories is about making an effort to generate more cheerful energy and participating in events that excite. Even the latest statistics about tourism state that people want an experience when they travel. They want to return home and tell others all about the things they saw and accomplished. They want to extend themselves and have adventures that release endorphins, are challenging, that teach them something and increase their joy. Travelling the distance together in a relationship needn't be any different. Other benefits generated by taking part in intrepid journeys are that they make awesome dinner party fodder and wildly interesting social media posts.

It's all about letting lightness in and not allowing the heaviness of everyday life to drag us down. Yes, mortgages are real and dinner has to be cooked. Lawns need to be mowed, bills have to be paid on time, children need to get to their activities, and work eats up a major part of our existence, all of which just makes it even more important to have fun in our downtime.

Secret number 76: Relationships are strengthened by romance, fun, and adventure.

Experiencing joy and releasing endorphins has an added bonus. When your brain perceives happiness, it eases muscle tension and improves digestion. So not only does a smile improve your looks, but your outlook.

We are role models for future generations. Young people learn more from what they see us doing, than from what we say. Even if you don't have children of your own, you can still act as though you are one. Play is not just for small people. Young people want parents and other grown-ups to have water pistol fights, read nonsense rhymes, and picnic on the lounge floor. It gives them hope that life can continue to be fun when he or she grows up. They want you to join in and ride the luge rather than sit on the sideline. They want you to wear a pirate costume complete with a parrot on your shoulder, an eye patch and an accent to match, and walk the plank at their birthday party. They would like you to have a themed birthday of your own, and they want to see the photographs that prove you sat on a toadstool dressed as a princess with all your friends, eating fairy sprinkle sandwiches and blowing bubbles. They don't want you sitting on the couch at Halloween; they want you at the door, in a scary costume, handing out fake chicken feet, plastic spiders and sweets, with a blackened tooth or two. They want you as their aunt or sister or friend to make swords out of cardboard or sticks and have you eagerly challenge imaginary creatures, dinosaurs, dragons, and devils in disguise.

In our relationships, having dangerous and daring adventures means not having everything overly controlled or planned. Uncertain outcomes are stimulating. I'm not suggesting that you rush out and wrestle a crocodile, or jump out of a perfectly good aeroplane unless you really, really want to. Perhaps just aim for simple ways you can show courage and be open to risk.

It could be that you simply choose to eat out somewhere new. You could make cool culinary choices like eating your way through a row of Asian eateries in the city. Every Sunday for ten Sundays on a set budget of $10 each, work your way through each and every restaurant without exception, even those perilous ones where they bring fire to the table so that you can cook things yourself.

Plan a weekend away in the country with pleasant company. Go with family or friends that sparkle and lavish you with songs and stories. Treat the boys to a trout fishing morning complete with guide, where they learn to cast, catch and release, and come home with tales between their tongues. Secretly pre-book a wild adventure to somewhere like a corn evil maze. Navigate your way there through dark fog-filled country lanes, and fill your evening with pushing and shoving, ducking and diving, and cries of, "No, you go first!" Make the night so scream-filled and riotous that you end up with cramp in your cheeks from laughing so much.

- Build an outdoor fire.
- Skim stones.
- Explore rock pools.
- Sleep under the stars.
- Visit an underground wine cellar.
- Swim in a swimming hole.
- Eat chilli hotter than you think you can handle.
- Eat something you caught yourself.
- Eat something you grew yourself.

- Perform a duet at a Karaoke bar.
- Host your own wine tasting event with guests.
- Give each other a face pack and try not to smile.
- Climb a real mountain.
- Spice things up. Make a curry from scratch.
- Have a water balloon fight.
- Go cheese tasting and brave the stinky weird ones.
- Challenge each other to a target shooting competition.
- Race go-karts.
- Grab some small hotel room spirits, line up a variety of fruit, ice, herbs, juice and soda and make your own cocktails.
- Make a compost bin and worm farm.
- Make a snowperson.
- Run through sprinklers in a local park.
- Take your shoes off whenever possible.
- Stay up the whole night and watch at least one sunrise.
- Tell ghost stories.
- Touch something slimy.
- Go on, I dare you!

Seductive Siren Songs

From this day forward, promise to say, "I love you" once a week and really mean it. Your beloved isn't just someone you share a house, castle, or your time with. What you have is special. How about celebrating the uniqueness of your relationship by giving it its own distinctive elevated energy? Think of it like having your own love language, a way of being that is different to how you are with anyone else. Make your connection as beautiful as a flowery island surrounded by rocks and cliffs. Like all good seductive sirens, use your irresistible appeal to entice your beloved in, but keep your promises real.

Slow down and allow room for your loving feelings and words to surface. In order to dispel the myth that others must somehow magically know all the good things you feel about them, bravely share your tender thoughts. Convey love silently. Emit it through your eyes and seductively hold your gaze a little longer than usual.

Adopt this daily question: What am I doing today that brings us closer?

Offer this kind of love and encouragement and validate his or her positive qualities in a tender tone:

- You're really special to me.
- My life has so much more meaning with you in it.
- I'm glad you're a part of my life.
- You're wonderful to be around.
- I love how you are with the children.
- You have the most beautiful eyes.
- You look sexy in that.
- If we weren't already together, I'd ask for your phone number.
- I love how you think.

In our busy world, one day can often run into the next and before we all know it, we can go weeks without hearing anything lovely. That's why it's so important to affirm each other when the feeling strikes. It doesn't take much to look through affectionate, adoring eyes, and behave as though your love is new.

Secret number 77: Receiving compliments lifts your spirits. Give them generously.

If such validation doesn't come naturally, recall the original things you used to make a fuss about.

- What was it about your beloved that made you go all dough-eyed and gooey when you first met them?
- What made you sail past rocks to reach them?
- Try remembering what they have offered you spiritually, emotionally, physically, and intellectually, and watch their alluring qualities appear before you.

Important anniversaries are private milestones personal only to your relationship, so give yourself permission to celebrate them.

During celebrations:

- Talk about the love you used to feel and the promises you made to each other.
- Play: Remember when? Then watch the good feelings flood back.
- Treat each other with traditional gifts of love just because they bring pleasure. Think flowers, rings, fragrance, underwear, wine, chocolates, and hearts.

If money is tight:

- Attract his or her attention with an appeal that's hard to resist. Make a voucher that promises neck rubs and romantic candlelit dinners.

Forget about being sensible:

- Have a massive picnic in a meadow starred with flowers; take grapes, strawberries, melon, bananas, cherries, honey, and kissing chocolate.
- Feed each other. Concentrate on his or her mouth rather than your own, and watch any control fade away. Slow down and connect deeply, in between bouts of laughter.

Step outside your normal role:

- Be the dangerous and beautiful creature you are and lure your beloved with enchanting music and a sexy voice.
- Talk dirty from time to time, in private, and when they least expect it.
- Slip a sexy note into your beloved's pocket, briefcase, or into their suitcase if they travel often.
- Write love-notes in lipstick on the mirror, in chalk on the pavement, or on post-it notes in their diary. Chalk pens allow you to draw all over anything that's glass, and they clean off easily.

Secret number 78: The best recipe for success is couple's only time, at least one weekend every six months, and one week every year.

The more trouble a couple is in, the greater the likelihood is that they haven't spent quality time together (without work or children) in ages. Avoid lethargy. It's a common thread that weaves its wicked way into rocky relationships way too often.

- Plan and create one night away together without pressures and distractions.
- Break free of routine and welcome risk and adventure.
- Take the beeswax out of your ears and listen to songs of love.
- Try new things in order to connect in an intimate sensual way.
- Light candles and set the mood for loving. Kiss, play, and hold hands.
- Bathe or shower together and have fun scrubbing backs and soaping each other up.
- Be soft, and take time to barely touch each other with the lightest of feather touches.
- Make frequent promises of delights to come.
- Use respectful fantasy.
- List interesting places you would like to make love. Could it be in front of the fire, on the beach, in the water, in a field, on a boat, in a foreign country, on a fire escape, on a rooftop, in a midnight storm, or under the glow of the moon?

Magic at Every Turn

Ancient fairytales continue to weave their magic and surprise and delight us, even in these modern times. If we want love to spring forward from the depths and splash through our lifetime of love, we just need to invite in loads of little sparks of spontaneity.

Unpredictably breathes new life into boring routines. It adds excitement. There's always magic waiting. It hides around corners we never knew existed. In order to experience wonder and soak up blissful moments, we need to:

- be open to them;
- embrace the unknown;
- leave time and room in schedules for last minute invitations; and
- follow cravings, desires, and whims when they hit.

Who doesn't want to have wishes filled and true love fulfilled? Spontaneity doesn't just happen; we have to make it happen.

Secret number 79: Sharing time, intimacy, spaces, ideas, dreams, and adventures, keeps relationships strong.

Take turns to invent the next thing you could do as a couple when you have spare time, free evenings, date nights, or weekends away. Pin your list up somewhere visible and tick things off as you do them. Be willing to discover dozens of blissful and invigorating ideas.

The well of ideas:

- Fondue night.
- Explore a farmers' market.
- Sit on a blanket, or find a park bench and have a picnic.
- Go for a long drive on a wild unexplored back road.
- Play a board game.
- Feed ducks.

- Go horse riding.
- Visit a real sweet shop.
- Play golf.
- Go taste-testing real chocolate, wine, or extra virgin olive oil.
- Try clay bird shooting.
- Ride a waterslide.
- Book a quad bike adventure.
- Watch re-runs of old movies and eat popcorn.
- Walk over a swing bridge, or through your local gardens.
- Build an outdoor bath and soak in fragrant bubbles under the stars.
- Take a train ride.
- Drive a tank.
- Visit a fun parlour.
- Squeeze into a photo booth and make foolish faces.
- Hunt down vintage treasure from your childhood.
- Go for a ride on a Harley.
- Draw pictures on the driveway in chalk, and then photograph them.
- Paint on canvas.
- Play with crayons on paper.
- Visit a fortune-teller.
- Make a talking stick.
- Hit the water in a kayak.
- Listen to a motivational speaker.
- Book a tandem massage.
- Go for a beauty treatment.
- Ride a ghost train.
- Eat food you have never tried before.
- Create a vision board that reflects how you want your future to look.
- Plant a special tree.
- Have a wild time at an amusement park.
- Ride a roller coaster and scare yourself silly.
- Collect treasure off a windswept beach.
- Visit zoo animals.
- Pat an elephant. One that is treated well.

- Play lawn bowls in your fancy white clothes.
- Swan from one hotel lobby to another, taste testing cocktails.
- Go for high tea.
- Watch a public fireworks display.
- Visit the botanical gardens.
- Walk and talk.
- Match your food, drink, movie and music with a country like France, Italy, India, South America or Spain, to add a global touch to a fun date night.
- Take surfing lessons.
- Play a game of darts.
- Take glow sticks, a blanket, and a flask of hot chocolate into your backyard and nestle into the night.
- Learn something tough or technical and cement your team spirit.
- Get your photo taken with a famous person.
- Fly a kite.
- Bake cookies.
- Try to spot a UFO, or at least a shooting star.
- Drink in a sunset.

Lust, love and laughter sprinkled through each day helps keep the flame alive and dancing.

Treats on the Treasure Trail

Small indulgences and delicacies needn't break the bank. How about lavishing each other with charm, words, and tiny trinkets that have heart value?

- Create many tiny fun times to look forward to and get excited about.
- Talk and laughter are free.
- Create conversations where you communicate your wishes, hopes, difficulties, and dreams. That doesn't cost anything at all.
- Share your thoughts and feelings, your interests and experiences.
- Ask for advice from each other now and again and be receptive.
- Establish regular rituals in your relationship.
- Remember small niceties like thank you and hello and goodbye.
- Kiss.
- Hug.
- Go to bed at the same time.
- Smile when you wake up.
- When you make yourself a drink, offer them one.

Talking about your passions cultivates the ones you have in common. Sometimes it helps to make a list of what you both adore, so you have a visual reminder of future activities. Think about including things like:

- art and exhibitions;
- interior design;
- tasting aromatic wines;
- learning more about horticulture;
- raising animals;
- attending workshops; and
- hunting for vintage treasures.

Secret number 80: Make time to treasure each other without distractions and exhaustion.

Keep finding things that you both love. Stay involved, interested, and present with each other. Something magical happens when you value the quality time you spend together. It provides instant proof that you rate your relationship highly.

- Read a magazine together. Choose one thing off each page that delights you.
- Window shop, and point out enchanting things of interest.
- Plan, brainstorm, and dream together.
- Read stories out loud to each other at bedtime.
- Enter competitions to win trips, dinner out, and tickets to events or movies so that you can surprise each other with treats.
- Review each other's latest creative work.
- Look at photographs that evoke happiness from your past.
- Barter your work if you can, to gift each other with a new experience.
- Dance, even if it's just in the kitchen.
- Hunt for a joke a day to share with each other.
- Design a treasure hunt for the next special occasion, and lead the way to the next clue with a mix of breadcrumbs and chocolate pebbles.
- Pick fruit at a roadside orchard and when you get home make something delectable from it.
- Drink fizz, eat potato chips, and yell loudly for the team of your choice.
- Plant a charming garden.
- Take a class and learn something fascinating.
- Learn a language.
- Go bike riding.
- Have a karaoke night.
- Shoot hoops.
- Raise an animal that brings joy into your world.
- Solve a mystery.
- Go hiking and use your wits to get out alive. Or take a compass!
- Redecorate a room. Make it captivating.
- Make sour dough bread. Cut a cross in the top to let any fairies escape before you bake it.
- Rekindle something old like a lamp or a coffee table.

- Make a play list of the songs you both love.
- Put a photo album together.
- Play mini golf.
- Prepare your own sushi.
- Create decorations or gift-wrap for the holiday season.
- Play petanque.
- Get out the beer, or ginger beer, turn on the grill, and build your own burgers.
- Make gingerbread people.
- Pitch a tent or teepee.
- Play old-fashioned noughts and crosses, hangman, or join the dots.
- Nail a crossword.
- Build something spectacular that you have always wanted, like a pizza oven, a fire pit or herb garden.
- Take up a challenge like making your own lunches for a week instead of buying them.
- Create enchanted spaces by stringing up fairy lights or vintage lighting.
- Perfect a new recipe.
- Paint something at a ceramics studio.
- Take up an activity like golf, tennis, scrabble, or knitting.
- Satisfy your sweet tooth and make homemade candy.

Toasty, Comfy, and Cosy

As much as toasty, comfy, and cosy may sound like the sort of names the seven little people in the *Snow White* tale might choose if they wanted to become ten little people, this isn't about adding to their hard working clan. It's more about finding nice words to encourage you to choose to rest for a few hours when rest and rejuvenation are needed. Staying refreshed makes mood management possible. Late nights, stressful events, and lack of sleep can turn us into Grumpy, Dopey and Sleepy far too easily, making it so much more difficult to assemble rational judgement or choose calm emotional responses. Naps take us on small vacations that lead to clear thinking and loving behaviours. Small rests are emotionally effective and will have you waking up more refreshed than Sleeping Beauty's one hundred years of fully conked out sleep.

Goldilocks may have been the only character that actually slept healthily in the fairytale world without being tricked into it by someone wicked.

A word of warning if you are feeling a little sleepy, reading the following brief explanation of *Goldilocks* may induce tiredness!

Goldilocks found a cute unlocked cottage in the woods and went inside to have a bit of a nosey. Being the type of girl who couldn't restrain herself, she tasted and ate her way through *The Three Bear's* plates of porridge before deciding she was a little tired. That's when she went in search of the living room chairs. She would have slept in Baby Bear's chair, except for the fact that it was too small and it broke. By then she was desperate for a lie down, so she went upstairs and lay down in all of the bear's beds until she found the most comfortable one of all; the small one. She fell fast asleep and stayed that way until Momma Bear, Papa Bear and Baby Bear returned home and chased her out.

The bears, who we could also rename toasty, comfy, and cosy due to their gorgeous fur coats, were thankfully good natured about the whole business and responded in a fairly civilized manner despite the fact that *Goldilocks* went about getting her own way like a juvenile delinquent. Frightening her away was a suitable consequence because she shouldn't have intruded or played around with property that didn't belong to her.

Goldilocks demonstrates that:

- Even when there isn't a clear solution to a difficulty, we can still learn something about ourselves in the process.
- What we choose to be attracted to warrants further investigation. Why are we drawn to certain things and certain behaviours? What is it about them that our character identifies with?
- The privacy of others always needs to be respected.
- Sometimes we need to take healthy rests without being afraid of upsetting others.
- We could do with being gentle on those who daydream.
- When we take our time making decisions, we make better choices.

Secret number 81: Relaxing makes room for new ideas to surface, intuition to rise, and greatly enhances creativity.

What are you waiting for? Rest easy.

- Find a big puffy bed, take off your shoes and have a snuggle-fest in some high thread-count sheets.
- Use a beautifully soft wheat-filled bag to cover your eyes and shut out the light.
- Leave empty spaces in your schedule.
- Read a book that's easy to escape into.
- Soak your feet in a basin of fragrant warm water.
- Engage in people watching.
- Breathe deeply and slowly into your belly, not your chest.
- Try alternate nostril breathing to gain clarity.
- Lie on the grass, spread your arms and legs out, and watch the sky float by.
- Listen to music that moves you.
- Soak in a spa or hot pool.
- Sit outside and just do nothing.
- Embrace stillness.

Make time to

Burst a cherry tomato in your mouth

Stop and make a wish

Dream while you do the dishes

Welcome your reflection

Gaze into your beloved's eyes

LISTEN TO YOUR INTUITION

Watch ants crawl

Calmly follow instructions

Notice the beat of your heart

Listen to melodic bird song

Watch children grow

Pleasantly thank those who help you

Appreciate what your body is saying

Feel lust deep within your bones

Laze in bed on weekend mornings

Watch a sunset change shades

Observe a snail's pace

Delight your 10,000 tastebuds

WAIT FOR YOUR PORRIDGE TO COOL

Diamonds and Toads

Diamonds and Toads is an old French fairytale about two sisters, both treated very differently by their greedy mother. The youngest was pretty, courteous and kind, but because she looked so much like her late father she was cruelly treated. The eldest sister looked and behaved more like her mother; selfish, ugly, and mean-spirited, so she became the favoured one. One day an old woman at a well asked the youngest daughter for a drink, to which the girl responded with natural kindness and compassion. For being so nice, she was rewarded with having either a diamond or a pretty flower fall from her mouth whenever she spoke. Enraged that this should happen to her least favourite daughter, the mother forced the other daughter to go and find the same old woman. She did, and of course was naturally rude and insulting to the old woman who happened to be a magic fairy especially disguised to test the characters of mortals. Not liking the nasty girl's character very much, she made toads and snakes fall from the girl's mouth. The mother gave up and threw both daughters out of the house. The youngest met a handsome prince and married him, and the eldest daughter was, shall we say, less fortunate.

The girl's behaviour is a classic example of the important message in Jon Kabat-Zinn's fabulous book *Wherever You Go, There You Are*. Wherever they went, they took their natural selves with them, which of course meant they ended up with two very distinct and different consequences. The magic fairy served as a reminder, that kind speech and empathy is rewarded, and less than fabulous behaviour isn't.

There's no doubt that the parenting style of the mother left a lot to be desired. This tale and one of its messages is very similar in style to *Cinderella,* that despite crappy treatment we can still choose to be full of sparkle and delight, ever hopeful for better times.

So many theories rightly say that:

- we yearn for what was missing when we were growing up; or
- we find ways to just let the missing qualities shine within us; and
- if nothing was missing growing up, we yearn for what we did get and miss getting now.

Children are such wide-eyed, innocent, beautiful creatures who seem to know from an early age how they want to be loved. They want more than protection and provisions, they want to be truly emotionally cared for. Being abandoned in the wilderness because you don't comply with the expectations of a crabby mother is pretty harsh. Abandonment is a common fairytale theme, look at *Hansel and Gretel*; they were thrown out into the woods when their parents ran out of food.

Parents and caregivers number one priority is to nurture and approve of who their child is. Children love it when we pay attention to them, when we marvel at their talents, and we let them know we are genuinely surprised at their capabilities. The same needs are still present when we grow up. We still want nurturing and approval whatever our age. Whilst the ideal is to nurture and approve of ourselves, we also shine a little brighter when people tell us we're amazing.

> *"Being deeply loved by someone gives you strength,*
> *while loving someone deeply gives you courage."*
> **Lao Tzu.**

When you observe the kind of connection that some people have and others long for, loving deeply is the key. We all want validation. To validate is to love deeply.

Secret number 82: Marvel at your beloved's talents. Express genuine surprise and delight at their capabilities.

Fear of rejection often sits right alongside love. To stay more on the lasting side of love requires us to promote the talents of our loved ones. Be brave, inquisitive, and verbal. Notice their sparkle, be aware of their cut, clarity, and colour, and let him or her know you notice their many multifaceted ways of shining brilliantly.

Secret number 83: To love, to love fully, to love deeply, requires that you hearten, that you raise their spirits, back them up, and uplift and inspire.

The recipient of such love feels strengthened and sustained. It gives him or her more resolve to believe in themselves and helps them advance in positive ways.

You don't have to give real diamonds to consolidate a promise of forever. You can create enough brightness through validating, to light your hearts and the entire night sky.

When you uplift and inspire, the glow reflected back is bright enough to illuminate your own path forward. Imagine the potential when you are both buoyant and assured; it makes for a confident walk in the direction of your shared dreams.

Secret number 84: Love deeply. Substantiate, support, and strengthen all of the incredibly wonderful things that make your beloved who they are.

- Back up beliefs.
- Validate views.
- Foster friendship.
- Remain respectful.
- Cultivate creativity.
- Understand.
- Embrace.
- Encourage.
- Enliven
- Praise.
- Confirm greatness.
- Welcome growth.
- Uphold ideas.
- Advance actions.
- Consent to crazy notions.
- Affirm.
- Agree.
- Defend them fiercely.

Choose to be fascinated curious and intrigued.

Pied Piper to the Rescue

The chances of you being riddled with vermin that need to go on a one-way vacation are hopefully non-existent. Things needn't get that awful to tempt you to have some whimsical time out in a joyous town. Don't be led away! Plan a retreat somewhere inspirational, enriching and uplifting.

The Pied Piper of Hamelin is a Brothers Grimm fairytale about a flamboyantly dressed piper who was a professional rat-catcher. He rescued of the town of Hamelin and led their millions of rats away with his golden magic flute. When the townspeople refused to pay him what he was rightly due, he punished them by luring all the children away, never to return.

As tragic as the tale is, there is thankfully a lovely deeper meaning to be had. Family is more important than money, and without playfulness and creativity, life can appear empty and boring.

If:

- outside pressures begin to overtake your internal calm;
- you can't remember the last time you had fun;
- life feels a little too hum-drum; or
- your stress begins to impact on the quality of your relationship.

Rescue yourself and opt for:

- terrific time-out;
- scenery that's sun-filled and sizzling;
- relaxation;
- recreation;
- gooey affection;
- adventure that tickles the child within;
- delightful day dreams;

- frisky fun; and
- expansive horizons.

Hopefully some of those ideas will have an attractive musical ring to it that's perhaps worth following.

Be led towards desirable rather than disastrous events. Attend something out of the ordinary like:

- An art show.
- A car race.
- An air show.
- A butterfly farm.
- A harvest lunch.
- A comedy festival.
- A music festival.
- A craft fair.
- A book launch.
- An ice and snow carnival.
- A Hay House workshop, especially *I Can Do It!*
- A lantern festival.
- A chartered fishing trip.

Destination dates:

- Think seaside location. Go for beach walks, go fishing, build sandcastles, search for treasure, and dine on sumptuous seafood.
- Go camping, or stay somewhere simple with alternative power supplies.
- Aim for a touristy thing like a cultural show, or visit a famous local attraction.
- Scare yourselves silly in a haunted venue.
- With a bit of effort, a cookbook and dress up clothes, you could have a perfectly fun, exotic, pretend vacation at home.

If you have trouble deciding between camping and five-star comforts, then blindfold yourself and fire a dart at one of the following:

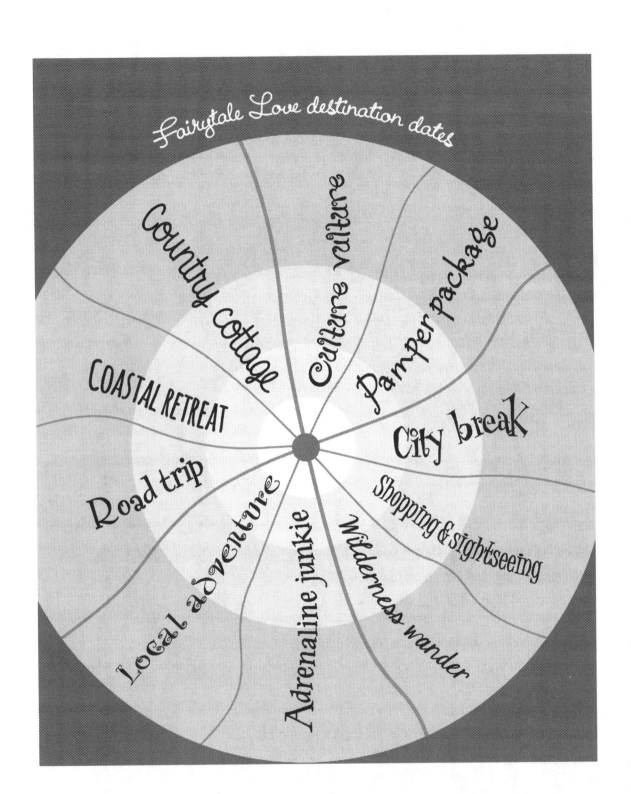

Fairytale Love destination dates

Culture vulture
Pamper package
Country cottage
City break
COASTAL RETREAT
Shopping & sightseeing
Road trip
Wilderness wander
Local adventure
Adrenaline junkie

Jack, the Giant Killer

All beanstalks need staking if they are to reach their full potential, just as all relationships require support if they are expected to grow.

Jack and the Beanstalk is an old British fairytale where Jack swapped a cow (which he was supposed to sell) for magic beans, which angered his mother, who threw them outside. When Jack woke up the following morning he saw they had produced a beanstalk that grew right up into the sky. He climbed all the way up to the very top and saw a beautiful castle. In the castle was a kind-hearted giant's wife who took a shine to him. She fed Jack and protected him from her monster of a husband on both his visits; despite the fact she knew he was a light-fingered trickster. On Jacks third visit he stole a magical golden harp that alerted the giant to his presence. Jack hi-tailed it down the beanstalk calling for his mother to bring him an axe. He chopped the beanstalk down just in the nick of time, and the giant was never seen again. When Jack showed his mother the stolen gold, the golden hen that laid golden eggs, and the talking golden harp, she chose to reward his cleverness rather than punish him for stealing and murdering. They became rich, Jack married a beautiful princess, and they all lived happily ever after. Well everyone except the giant and his kind wife.

There was a lot of gifting going on in *Jack and the Beanstalk*. The magician gifted Jack with magic beans, the giant's wife gifted Jack with food and kindness, and the stolen goods gifted Jack and his mother with riches. And let's not forget, the riches gifted Jack with a very good chance of scoring a gorgeous wife.

Speaking of gorgeous, on the *Oprah* show, the very beautiful and influential American businesswoman, writer and heiress Ivanka Trump was asked a giant-size question. "What was the biggest gift your parents have ever given you?" She didn't say gold, she didn't say treasure or trinkets, she didn't say magic beans, and she didn't say fame, fortune, or opportunity. Without blinking an eyelid Ivanka said, "Love and accessibility."

Whether it's a beanstalk or a ladder one climbs to success, it's important we remember to make time to love, and that we stay open to being loved. Work often lures us away from those closest to us. Avoidance, being inattentive, or maintaining an illusion of being together when we are in fact distracted, are some of the ways disconnection shows up in relationships.

It's possible that disconnection also stems from a fear of loss. Wherever there is love, loss inevitably follows. Until death do us part is a natural occurrence that we mustn't dwell on. How crazy would it be if fear won out? Love no matter what.

The giant's wife displayed a form of disconnection by choosing to repeatedly lie to him. She said there was no boy in the castle despite her husbands repeated chant of:

> ***"Fee-fi-fo-fum,***
> ***I smell the blood of an Englishman,***
> ***Be he alive, or be he dead,***
> ***I'll have his bones to grind my bread."***

The giant's wife, like Jack and his mother, was dealing with adversity. They were all finding the best ways to cope in difficult circumstances.

Serious ways that disconnection can manifest:

- game-playing;
- control;
- addiction;
- abandonment;
- anger;
- violence;
- neglect; and
- ogre-like bullying.

Less damaging ways it can show up is through:

- disinterest;
- disappearing;
- acting invisible;

- blame;
- martyrdom;
- over-functioning;
- under-functioning; or
- losing oneself in technology, work, or problems.

Connecting is worth the effort.

Love and be loved.

Turn towards each other and conjure up complimentary communication. It creates a nice atmosphere in your relationship. Perhaps if the giant had displayed a kinder temperament it may have made it easier for his wife to share that she liked having company over. She may have told him that even though he might want to eat little boys up, she preferred them alive, for conversation purposes.

Secret number 85: What you give out, you get back. What you nurture, not only survives, it eventually thrives.

Kindness yields immense benefits and contributes to your mutual growth. Other qualities that are beneficial are:

- friendship;
- open-hearted communication;
- sincerity;
- equality;
- minimal expectations;
- honesty;
- doing your best to understand and be understanding;
- maturity;
- patience;
- appreciation;
- support; and
- a good balance of power.

Midnight Feasts, Pillow Fights, and Other Essential Adventures

- Ride a roller coaster.
- Bungy jump.
- Parasail.
- Fly somewhere exotic.
- Plan a perfect romantic evening.
- Play non-electronic games.
- Temporarily change your identity.
- Wear a wig.
- Hire a fabulous gown or suit.
- Wear fancy dress.
- Get your astrological chart drawn up.
- Go bush.
- Spend time with a baby.
- Go whale watching.
- Swim with dolphins.
- Go camping.
- Sail on a yacht.
- Dine on a launch.
- Have a picnic in a dinghy.
- Cook for a chef.
- Have a chef cook for you.
- Drink expensive champagne.
- Drink cheap bubbles.
- Drink a spider; it's delicious and simply made from ice cream and soda.
- Star gaze.
- Play singstar.
- Attend the ballet.
- Go to the theatre.
- Watch a dance troupe perform.
- Throw a huge party.

- Throw a tiny party.
- Say yes to fabulous invitations.
- Lose yourself in some serious bargain hunting.
- Hire a convertible for a day.
- Throw money into a fountain and make a wish.
- Ride a bicycle.
- Be photographed or filmed professionally.
- Fulfil an ambition.
- Send a love poem.
- Swim naked.
- Climb a mountain.
- Learn a new craft.
- Ski or snowboard.
- Tame a toboggan.
- Make a snowman and a snow angel.
- Sell your wares at a local fair.
- Throw a dress-up party.
- Make love on a fluffy rug in front of a crackling open fire.
- Raise money for charity.
- Donate to a worthy cause.
- Support a child's creativity, hobby, or passion.
- Ride a motorbike, or a scooter.
- Give blood and save a life.
- Become an organ donor.
- Have a full body massage.
- Stay the night in a luxury hotel.
- Sleep over in an inexpensive cabin.
- Sleep in a tent.
- Wish upon a shooting star.
- Spend time on a tropical island.
- Care for an animal.
- Build a tree house.
- Go fishing.
- Dance around a fire.
- Sing at the top of your lungs.

Mad Hatter Tea Party Topics

You don't have to wear foolish attire, but please partake of conversation topics that at least aren't dire, if you don't want your relationship to tire.

Spin the handle of a teapot and answer these questions:

- What **1** thing are you still looking for in life?
- What **2** countries would you like to visit and why?
- Which **3** memories are you most grateful for?
- What are your **4** favourite foods from childhood?
- If you could have **5** other lives what would you do in them?
- If you could bring someone back to life who would it be and why?
- Who would you choose as your ideal dinner party companions?
- What is your backwards name?
- What other life experiences do you most want to have?
- Describe your dream holiday.
- Who would you like meet in Wonderland?
- If you were given ten million dollars, what would you do with it?
- If you could have any job in the world, what would it be?
- How would you make the world a better place if you could?

Talk about which one you would rather be, and why, from the following topics:

- The river or the sea.
- A nose or a flower.
- The sun or the moon.
- A cat or a dog.
- A time traveller or an astronaut.
- A sheep or a cow.
- A highway or a country road.
- A dolphin or a whale.
- Night or day.

- Man or woman.
- A goblin or a ghoul.
- Summer or winter.
- A painting or a sculpture.
- March Hare or a Dormouse.

Pretend that you are a famous person, or an animal, and get your beloved to guess who or what you are:

- I look a bit like...
- I sound rather like...
- I smell a bit like...
- I feel (to touch) a bit like...
- I laugh rather like...
- I move quite a bit like...

Talk about the fairytales you remember the most from childhood:

- Which character did you most identify with?
- Who was the scariest?
- Who was the most beautiful?
- Who was the most atrocious?
- Which characters remind you of people in your life?
- Which fairytale is most like your life?
- Which characters would you love to have been?
- What do you think certain fairytales taught you?
- What magic power would you most like to have and why?

Play pin the grin on the Cheshire cat.

How to Work Magic

We don't need a sorcerer's cloak, or even a magic wand. What we actually need is a heart of a gold, spare time, and a belief in goodness. Because economic times seem to be getting tougher for a lot of people, why not look at the things we have that could be traded, gifted, or offered to others in need.

There's something thrilling and magical that occurs when we begin to simplify and strip back, and when we aim to live with essentials rather than wasting resources. Even surrounding ourselves with natural beauty can create mysterious calm when things are chaotic. When we diminish physical and emotional clutter, we gain more peace within. Serenity enables us to look outward, to create harmonious solutions for our relationships and our exquisite environment.

We must never waste the wonderful gift of life. Beyond loving, the formula to fulfilment consists of knowing we are here for a purpose, and then using that purpose for the greater good. We can be of service to humanity in many different sized ways.

Secret number 86: Your life becomes better by making other people's lives better.

- Be a surprise in disguise for someone in need.
- Be a good fairy and secretly grant someone a wish.
- Go ahead and nurture others.
- Practise the art of giving, just because you can.
- Bake someone you love a beautiful birthday cake.
- Invite a friend over for a home cooked meal.
- Make a huge pot of soup and deliver half of it to an elderly neighbour.
- Turn your trash into someone's treasure.
- Reduce. Reuse. Recycle.
- Make sure your car is fuel-efficient.
- Buy less stuff.

- Buy products from socially responsible companies.
- Conserve water and energy.

If you have anything that you no longer need, pass it on to an organization that specifically collects items for people in need.

- Furniture, toys, and bedding are welcomed at women's refuge organizations, or single parent centres.
- Children in need can always do with shoes, backpacks, and books.
- The homeless appreciate food, blankets and sleeping bags.
- Animal sanctuaries are thankful for farm supplies, adoptions, finances, and physical help.
- Foster children prefer using suitcases rather than plastic bags when they have to move around.
- Toys, clothes, and books, are great for people who have to relocate after losing everything.
- Some organizations collect things like medicine and prescription glasses to send to disadvantaged countries.

One small gift from many can help enormously. Work your magic. You may not have the ability to control or predict the natural world, but you may be able to donate a small amount of money to help. $1 donated by a million people is a million dollars, which can help a community immensely.

After floods, fires, and earthquakes, people sometimes don't even have underwear of their own. If you have your own company, have you ever considered how you could make someone else's day by passing on what you no longer need? Leftovers can be ever so helpful for hungry animals. Even tiny morsels can be shared. Birds and hedgehogs seem ever so grateful for scraps of food.

- Donate a blanket or food parcel to an organization that supports those who are less fortunate.
- What about offering your services as an auction item?
- Some towns need volunteers for civil defence or fire fighting.

- You could read out loud to someone with poor eyesight.
- Volunteer in an animal shelter, or soup kitchen.
- Befriend an elderly person.
- Older people sometimes find it difficult to clean their gutters and change smoke alarm batteries and could appreciate the offer of help.
- What about feeding someone's pet when they go away, or cutting your neighbour's lawn if they aren't able to?
- Subscribing to an organization that focuses on a cause close to your heart can be a great thing to do if you don't have the time to contribute in other ways. There are many awesome passionate action groups out there that stop destructive progress in the world, that practise conservation, and do wonders for endangered species.
- Save all the living creatures in the sea by using less plastic.
- Save the whales. Even though they are gigantic, they really need you on their side.

Surprise someone today:

- Practise a random act of kindness.
- Secretly help someone in need.
- Leave goodies on their doorstep.
- Gift them with wild flowers.
- Be an inspiration.
- Share a brainstorming session and give loads of ideas away for free.
- Swap your talent for their talent.
- Swap your product for their services.
- Barter when you have the opportunity.
- Purchase a coffee for someone who can't afford one of his or her own.
- Champion a business you believe in.
- Use social media to brag about people who are awesome.
- Be a mentor.
- Gift your physical labour.
- Share excess fruit and vegetables growing in your garden.
- Offer your babysitting services.
- Teach someone an easier way to do something.

Inside your relationship, be as generous:

- Hug, listen, and care.
- Make his or her vehicle sparkle.
- Do one of the chores that you know he or she has been avoiding.
- Cook them something delicious.

What interests those close to you? Write down the kinds of things you know that other people love, and call on the list when it is gift-giving time, or when someone needs cheering up. Here are some small surprises that could easily fit into an envelope:

- Movie tickets.
- Book vouchers.
- Stamps.
- Phone credit.
- Petrol vouchers.
- Face packs.
- Hair clips.
- Photographs.
- Memory cards.
- Hot chocolate sachets.
- Herbal tea bags.
- A child's drawing.
- Music vouchers.
- Fairy dust.
- Inspirational sayings.
- A magnetic photograph.
- Poetry.
- A story.
- A scrumptious recipe.
- A handwritten letter.

Delightful Treats in Gumdrop Forest

"Never follow anyone else's path, unless you're
in the woods and you're lost and you see a path,
and by all means you should follow that."
Ellen deGeneres.

How often do we get lost in the woods, not able to find the right path? Sometimes it's helpful to look at the road other successful people are on, to help inspire and lead us towards our own dream and passion fulfilment. There are instances when we just need to search harder for what we like. Other times it requires us to:

- place more emphasis on noticing the sorts of things we are drawn to;
- bravely go off the trail of conformity;
- have a willingness to explore, risk, and work out which of our adventures make us wiggle and squirm;
- notice which experiences stimulate a deeper desire; and
- recognize what resonates with the raw passion that lives within us.

Bite-sized pieces of daily inspiration feed our souls, fuel our fiery imaginations, and drive us forward on our own passionate paths.

No wonder *Hansel and Gretel* were mesmerized by the incredible array of lollies in gumdrop forest, they were literally starving to death. Although they found instantaneous pleasure in gobbling up the array of sugary goodness, it's interesting to consider that unless that particular activity held some kind of deeper meaning, was either filled with rich significance and importance, or it was completely in line with their core values, the act of eating gumdrops isn't likely to ever fire up their passion and purpose.

That doesn't mean that they, or we should ever stop exploring. Finding a gingerbread house may ignite a passion for architecture, a love of construction, fulfil an artistic idea, and encourage devotion towards craft, horticulture, or sweet making.

Inspiration is the act of reaching into an abundant source, breathing it in, drinking it in deeply, and allowing ourselves to be touched by someone else's beauty and brilliance in a way that allows our own creative desires to be triggered and released.

Inspiration evokes memories and whimsical thoughts, stimulates imagination, sparks original thoughts in our own heads and hearts, and propels us onto fun pathways that hopefully fulfil our dreams and destiny.

Refuse to become stagnant.

- Reach for the stars.
- Do.
- See.
- Listen.
- Smell.
- Move.
- Taste.
- Read books.
- Be coached.
- Be led.
- Be a leader.
- Find encouragement.
- Encourage others.
- Cheerlead.
- Eat delicious morsels.
- Allow music to touch your soul.

Whether you choose to trip over inspiration, or intentionally seek it out, trust that fascination is the key that beckons to us to step closer. Enthralment reminds us to:

- absorb beauty;
- to marvel at;
- to become enchanted by;
- to learn more; and
- to become further engaged in new possibilities.

Secret number 87: Welcome more laughter into your world.

Laughter:

- heats up a relationship;
- paves the path to intimacy;
- warms the emotional climate;
- binds people together;
- lightens the mood;
- loosens up situations; and
- energizes interactions.

Embrace your playful side:

- Buy Maurice Sendak's book *Where the Wild Things Are*. What talent! He was one of the greatest writers and illustrators of children's literature, ever. This inspirational book makes a great addition to every mischief-making grown-up's library.
- Tell jokes that are guaranteed to cause giggles. Like: Why don't cannibals eat clowns? Answer: Because they taste funny!
- Play uncomplicated card games, like *Snap* and *Memory*.
- Rent a ridiculous movie. Actors like Will Ferrell, Whoopi Goldberg and Jim Carey are masters of nonsense.
- Wear a wolf suit, a chicken suit, or dress like a princess for dinner.
- Find a mythical creature and stare into its yellow eyes without blinking once.
- Wear a stick on tattoo. Put it somewhere that only you or your beloved can see.
- Serve up children's party food at the next grown-up party you host.
- Spit watermelon pips or olive stones, and measure the distance they travel.
- Roll in fresh dew on a soft lawn.
- Close your eyes and see how many steps you can take before you have to open them.
- Howl at the next full moon.
- Serve up cups of tea in child-size tea sets.
- Wear bare feet and squish around in the mud.
- Let the wild rumpus begin.
- Have a monster party.

- Finger paint.
- Dance until you are too hot to keep your clothes on.
- Wear your best outfit just because you want to.
- Get naked for no particular reason.
- Wear a tail.
- Take your camera for a walk and view the world from a new angle.
- Wear a weird hat.
- Go boogie boarding and squeal loudly.
- Return home and eat your supper.

Secret number 88: Support people and things that inspire you, fill you with delight, and cause you to giggle contagiously.

Keep your eyes open to what's going on in the world:

- Google a topic you want to learn more about.
- Discover, then bookmark your most uplifting websites.
- Fill your bookshelves with inspiring books.
- Go to libraries, design stores, galleries, museums, art fairs, wearable art shows, and exhibition centres.

Read fabulous blogs like:

- Fairytale Love. www.leannefrench.com
- www.wolfies.co.nz
- www.hayhouseoz.wordpress.com
- www.gemsofgorgeousness.com
- www.jaredgulian.com
- www.lisaselow.com
- www.purposefairy.com
- www.tinybuddha.com

Consume creativity:

- Start with www.etsy.com

- www.felt.co.nz

Soak up knowledge from an expert that could help someone else down the track:

- Listen to relationship expert Dr. John Gottman on YouTube.
- Listen to www.ted.com for riveting talks by remarkable people.
- Learn from a sexpert. www.drlauraberman.com
- Find out about emotional abuse, power and control, domestic violence, workplace bullying, school bullying and more from Dr. Clare Murphy. www.speakoutloud.net

Stay inspired:

- Jamie Oliver's DVD collection just makes you want to cook outdoors.
- Collect decadent, delightful cookbooks.
- Go on a food tour with passionate foodies. www.gourmetjoy.co.nz
- Learn something new.
- Play beautiful music.
- Research a dream holiday destination. Start saving.
- Subscribe to your favourite magazines and eagerly await their delivery.
- Read literature that feeds your mind, body, and spirit.
- Read children's books that fill you with delight. Smile! Starring Sunny McCloud by Leigh Hodgkinson is adorable.
- Get your numerology chart done. www.michellebuchanan.co.nz
- Heal your life. www.louisehay.com
- Master the art of manifesting. www.drwaynedyer.com
- Read *Happiness Now!* By Robert Holden.
- Live your best life. www.oprah.com
- Cultivate compassion. www.pemachodronfoundation.org
- Dream, dare, and do. www.planetsark.com
- Find the courage to be vulnerable. www.brenebrown.com
- Book yourself an astrological yearly forecast or a relationship report. www.astrologyhouse.co.nz
- Delve into divine magic with Doreen Virtue. www.angeltherapy.com
- Vintage lingerie, lovely linens, bespoke garments. www.SharonaCraig.etsy.com
- Embrace sacredness. www.deniselinn.com

- Change your life with a bestselling author. www.cherylrichardson.com
- Get motivated by The Feel Good Fairy. www.heatherbestel.com
- Find an object or illustration from your childhood that encapsulates make-believe, mystery, or magic, and be re-inspired by it.
- Create pockets of beauty on windowsills, bookshelves, and desks.
- Watch quality, innovative, non-fiction television. www.jamtv.co.nz
- Fan the creative spark that lives within. Produce your own wonders.
- Stay curious. Be open to all avenues of creativity even the burlesque and hip. www.gutsandgarters.tumblr.com/ https://www.facebook.com/gutsandgarters www.dinosaur-toast.tumblr.com/
- Transform your space. Lovingly re-purpose a piece of furniture.
- Cut out pictures that spark your ideas. Paste them into scrapbooks.
- Adorn your body with handmade silver, acrylic, and resin goodies from a range of jewellery called Wonderland, Summer Sprinkles & The Diamond Diaries. www.feijoadesigns.co.nz
- Buy art from galleries that represent artists with integrity. www.orexart.co.nz
- Enlist great PR help to get your talent or product out into the world. www.impactpr.co.nz and http://www.thorntoncomms.co.nz/
- Devour everything Dr Seuss has ever written.
- Eat cupcakes.
- Get a really great massage. Judy Livingstone from www.massageinmartinborough.gen.nz is amazing. Sheelagh O'Dowd in Auckland is an excellent Hellerwork practitioner. Naomi Cassrels is a great massage therapist in Dubai.
- Support, attend, and celebrate movies from your own country.
- Dine at eateries that excite. Move away from blandness.
- Be sure to search online for Jim Cooper's ceramic sculptures.
- Celebrate mermaids. https://www.facebook.com/vintagemermaid.nz
- Sleep in beautiful linen fit for a princess. www.frontroomfabrics.co.nz
- Loose yourself in a mosaic sculpture garden. Stay the night in a beautifully themed room. www.thegiantshouse.co.nz

- Take an art class with a fun artist. http://brendanmcgorry.com/
- Go on a farm tour, pat cute animals and buy jams and preserves. www.martinboroughmanner.co.nz
- Walk into fashion Wonderland where they believe in the magic of creativity and playing dress-ups. www.trelisecooperwellington.co.nz
- Read poetry. Especially Mary Oliver's.

Support local, handmade, independent producers and makers.

- www.sandrajanesuleski.co.nz
- http://www.behance.net/BodineSaari
- https://www.facebook.com/carolinefrenchart
- www.redbarnart.mattguild.com
- http://www.martygirl.com
- www.emmamakes.com
- www.tirohanaestate.com
- Buy from artisan producers. www.purewairarapa.co.nz
- The wonderful world of wine. http://terroir-wines.co.nz/

Follow these fabulous folk with a fairytale slant on Facebook:

- Mister Finch. His work will make you squeal with delight. https://www.facebook.com/MisterFinchTextileArt
- THE IMAGINARIUM. https://www.facebook.com/YscHome
- Soju Shots. https://www.facebook.com/konbae
- Edge City. https://www.facebook.com/pages/Edge-City/182139440044
- Gladys Paulus felt artist. https://www.facebook.com/GladysPaulusFeltArtist
- Felting Dreams by Johanna Molina. https://www.facebook.com/FeltingDreamsByJohanaMolina

Always stay inspired, love your magnificent self, keep respect at the forefront, think before you act, stay emotionally honest, pursue playfulness, get excited about the goodness that lies within, **reach out** to the vulnerable person you love, and watch your happiness increase tenfold.

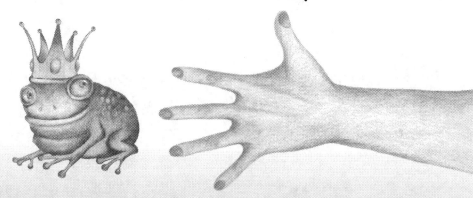

Until the end of time... love, laugh, and remember that a frog is just a prince in disguise.

"Life is the most wonderful fairy tale of all."
Hans Christian Anderson.